The Human Side of School Leadership

We often talk about leadership as strategy, structure and outcomes – but what if the real work begins with how we treat each other?

This guide offers a deeply human exploration of what it means to lead schools where people truly matter. Drawing on years of coaching and wellbeing supervision with headteachers, CEOs and leadership teams, Shaheen Myers provides a powerful reimagining of leadership that places care, connection and courage at its core.

From 'Teach Me How to Treat You' and 'Carefrontations' to 'Performance Management', each chapter empowers leaders to cultivate a sense of belonging and resilience in their teams. Case studies, reflection exercises and insights from a range of leaders, including Mary Myatt (an education adviser, writer and speaker) and Sufian Sadiq (Director of Teaching School and Co-president Elect for Chartered College of Teaching), invite the reader to pause, reflect, and realign their values, asking:

- What happens when we lead with authenticity, not armour?
- How do we build cultures where people feel seen, valued, and safe?
- How can leaders sustain themselves while supporting everyone else?

Grounded in evidence, lived experience and empathy, this book will leave the reader feeling supported, valued and equipped to grow both personally and professionally. It is an essential resource for all senior leaders who are committed to creating thriving and supportive school communities.

Shaheen Myers is the founder of Balance:ed, an organisation dedicated to transforming school leadership through wellbeing, culture and connection. A former headteacher, executive leader, deputy director for a large local authority, coach and trusted adviser to multi-academy trusts, Shaheen works nationally with school and trust leaders to embed sustainable practices that prioritise people alongside performance.

The Human Side of School Leadership

How Courage, Connection and Care Transform Culture

Shaheen Myers

LONDON AND NEW YORK

Designed cover image: Getty Images

First published 2026
by Routledge
and by Routledge

4 Park Square, Milton Park, Abingdon, Oxon OX14 4RN
605 Third Avenue, New York, NY 10158

For Product Safety Concerns and Information please contact our EU representative GPSR@taylorandfrancis.com. Taylor & Francis Verlag GmbH, Kaufingerstraße 24, 80331 München, Germany.

Routledge is an imprint of the Taylor & Francis Group, an informa business

© 2026 Shaheen Myers

The right of Shaheen Myers to be identified as author of this work has been asserted in accordance with sections 77 and 78 of the Copyright, Designs and Patents Act 1988.

All rights reserved. No part of this book may be reprinted or reproduced or utilised in any form or by any electronic, mechanical, or other means, now known or hereafter invented, including photocopying and recording, or in any information storage or retrieval system, without permission in writing from the publishers.

Trademark notice: Product or corporate names may be trademarks or registered trademarks, and are used only for identification and explanation without intent to infringe.

British Library Cataloguing-in-Publication Data
A catalogue record for this book is available from the British Library

ISBN: 9781041003052 (hbk)
ISBN: 9781041002994 (pbk)
ISBN: 9781003609100 (ebk)

DOI: 10.4324/9781003609100

Typeset in Celeste
by Deanta Global Publishing Services, Chennai, India

For every leader and teacher who gives their all.
In memory of my late husband Rhys Myers, whose unconditional regard for others continues to guide this work.
For my grandson, Isaac – may he grow up guided by light, by example, and by care.
To my Nani – my first teacher of positive unconditional regard and how to lead fearlessly.

Contents

	Foreword by Steve Waters and Suneta Bagri	xi
	Acknowledgements	xvii
1	**Story of origin – my why**	1
	My story of origin	2
	Your why	9
	How to use this book	9
	Connecting questions	10
	Chapter summary	10
	Interludes	11
	Interlude 1, by Ann's reflection	12
2	**Care, connection and culture**	15
	Who we are beneath the titles	15
	The subtle shift from 'doing' wellbeing to 'being' well	16
	Belonging as the backbone of performance	18
	Turning existing practices into catalysts for change	19
	Reflection exercise	21
	Connection as the gateway to psychological safety	21
	Why staff surveys only scratch the surface	23
	The question that changes the conversation	25
	Reflection exercise	26
	Chapter summary	26
	Interlude 2, by Mary's reflection	28

Contents

3	**Teach me how to treat you**	31
	Moving beyond values lists	31
	Conversations that build connection and safety	32
	The science behind positive states of being	33
	Transforming meetings	33
	Small but significant acts of regard	34
	Bringing 'Teach me how to treat you' to education	35
	Colleagues who uplift us	36
	Colleagues who drain us	36
	The 'real' staff survey	37
	Case study: Whitechapel C of E Primary School – a culture shift from compliance to connection	40
	Reflection exercise	43
	Chapter summary	44
	Interlude 3, by Narinder's reflection	46
4	**Connecting questions and transforming meetings**	49
	Moving beyond superficial check-ins	49
	Psychological safety through connection	50
	Reflection exercise 1	50
	Reflection exercise 2	51
	Connecting questions of check-ins	52
	Five transformative connecting questions	53
	Let's take each question in turn	54
	Cultivating trust and openness	58
	Reflection exercise	60
	Chapter summary	61
	Interlude 4, by Sufian's reflection	62

Contents

5 Performance management: A shift worth making — 65
The reality behind the theory — 65
Questioning the status quo — 66
The role of intrinsic motivation — 68
From compliance to growth — 69
Professional development — 70
Balancing autonomy and accountability — 71
The power of MIQs in performance management — 73
The three most important questions — 73
Case study 1: Whitechapel C of E primary school – redefining performance management with MIQs — 75
Case study: Working with a CEO to transform executive team reflection — 78
Reflection exercise — 80
Chapter summary — 80

Interlude 5, by Andy's reflection — 82

6 Carefrontations: Enabling the hard conversations through psychological safety — 85
When the system gets in the way – navigating organisational tensions — 87
It's not revolutionary, it's relational — 88
The weight of unspoken tension – why we can't afford to ignore it — 89
Deepening team cohesion through time to think — 91
Coaching through limiting beliefs and emotional triggers — 93
Case study: Working with a CEO – reclaiming depth in executive conversations — 94
Saying a kind 'No' – boundaries as an act of care — 95
Boundaries are not barriers; they are clarity – and clarity is kind — 96
Reflection exercise — 98
Chapter summary — 98

Interlude 6, by Yamini's reflection — 100

Contents

7	**Headteachers: How to care for yourself when you're responsible for the welfare of all**	103
	The quiet weight of leadership	103
	Beneath the titles	104
	Models of leadership that reflect the real	104
	Support structures that truly support	105
	Values in action	106
	Guilt	107
	Enoughness over exhaustion	109
	A practical guide to looking after yourself (without the fluff)	110
	Finding self-efficacy: Redefining your role on your own terms	111
	Engaging in wellbeing coaching	112
	Example session	114
	Testimonials speak for themselves	115
	A personal offer to you	115
	Interlude 7, by Bushra's reflection	117
	Final reflections	119
	References	120
	Index	123

Foreword

The Human Side of School Leadership: How Courage, Connection and Care Transform Culture is a transformative guide for educational leaders seeking to create more human-centred, connected school environments. Shaheen Myers challenges traditional leadership approaches by emphasising vulnerability and emotional intelligence as essential tools for effective leadership. Born out of substantial educational experience, including as a headteacher and deputy director of education in a local authority, *The Human Side of School Leadership* serves as both a mirror and a roadmap for creating schools where everyone feels genuinely valued.

Shaheen introduces practical frameworks as given in the 'Connecting questions' features throughout her book to transform routine staff meetings into meaningful opportunities for collaboration and growth. Central to her philosophy is the concept of 'Teach me how to treat you' – encouraging leaders to articulate their own needs while creating psychological safety for others to do the same. Key themes include:
- how to ask for, and receive, respectful communication to create self-growth and psychological safety
- reimagining performance management as a process of personal development rather than compliance, and
- developing skills for 'carefrontation' – addressing conflicts with kindness and honesty, and providing essential self-care strategies for headteachers who carry enormous responsibility for their school communities.

Foreword

Rather than offering quick fixes, Shaheen's book advocates for a 'quiet revolution' in educational leadership – one that values deep thinking, authentic connection, and the recognition that behind every role is a human being deserving of respect and understanding. It is an invaluable roadmap for leaders who sense something vital is missing from their organisational mental wellbeing culture despite school policies on belonging and inclusion.

The publication *The Human Side of School Leadership* is timely: stress and burnout in the teaching profession have created a retention and recruitment crisis and there is an urgent need for whole-school mental wellbeing strategies to address it.

Introducing Shaheen's chapters

Chapter 1 establishes Shaheen's purpose in writing *The Human Side of School Leadership*, which is to open up a dialogue with the reader to find solutions to the challenges they face. Shaheen acknowledges the significant burdens carried by leaders, including loneliness, immense responsibility and constant pressure. The tension between the formality of their role and their humanity is acknowledged, as is the tendency of leaders to be seen as weak if they are open and honest about their vulnerabilities.

Shaheen invites us to revisit outdated models of leadership, to reconnect with why we set out on our teaching journey, and to rekindle empathy and authenticity in order to understand the lived experiences of those we lead.

Building on Chapter 1, in Chapter 2 Shaheen defines physical and mental wellbeing leadership as the culture leaders cultivate daily, rather than implementing disconnected wellbeing initiatives that have limited impact on the school. The three 'Cs' – Comparing, Complaining and Criticising – are defined as forces that reduce positivity and lower self-esteem. A 'C' that heals and elevates engagement and joy is Connection. Belonging should be a core driver of sustainable performance and organisational resilience. Leaders are invited to ask the important question 'Who are you beneath your role?'

Foreword

The key takeaway of Chapter 2 is that leadership is about creating a cultural mindset to build a psychological safe and connected school community.

Chapter 3 opens with a powerful question: How would I want to be encouraged right now? It asks us to pause and consider not just how we encourage others but how we, as leaders, wish to be treated. This simple but profound question lays the foundation for a philosophy that Shaheen argues is long overdue in education. Leaders and staff members often operate under assumptions about how to engage with one another. Addressing this question opens the door to vulnerability, respect and true connection. Educators and leaders are often so focused on their students and staff teams that they forget to articulate their own needs. Seeking a response to 'Teach me how to treat you' invites leaders to listen and define how others wish to be treated and how they would like to be treated themselves, to share that with their teams, transforming meetings and creating environments where everyone feels valued.

This chapter showcases a key theme in the book: the deep connection between personal wellbeing and leadership, and the importance of knowing how we wish to be treated so that we can respect and elevate the treatment of others. This theme is illustrated by a case study focusing on Whitechapel Church of England primary school (Cleckheaton, UK), which shifted from compliance-focused performance management to connection-based professional growth.

One of the most powerful tools in this book is the use of connecting questions to transform staff meetings into environments of growth and collaboration. In Chapter 4, the question 'Who or what makes you forget about time?' offers a glimpse into the deeper motivations and passions of the people we work alongside. In a world that is often focused on deadlines and data, this chapter reminds us of the importance of human connection and reflection.

As we reflect on our own personal experiences of school meetings, we gain insight into how to craft spaces where connection thrives and quality thinking flourishes. This chapter challenges us to reconsider the way meetings are conducted, providing practical strategies to ensure that everyone feels heard, valued and truly engaged. The chapter's

Foreword

central premise is deceptively simple yet profoundly challenging: that our everyday interactions – particularly our meetings – can become vehicles for building the deep sense of belonging that every organisation claims to desire. Rather than accepting the status quo of surface-level check-ins and agenda-driven gatherings, this chapter invites us to reimagine these moments as opportunities for authentic human connection.

In our rush to efficiency and productivity, we have inadvertently created cultures where thinking – real, deep, uninterrupted thinking – has become a luxury rather than a necessity. The framework presented here offers a path back to valuing not just the speed of our responses, but the quality of our thoughts and the depth of our understanding of one another. This chapter will resonate particularly with those who sense that something vital is missing from their organisational culture – that despite policies and strategies around belonging and inclusion, true connection remains elusive. It offers hope that transformation can begin with something as simple as asking better questions and creating safer spaces for the answers to emerge.

Performance management is often viewed as a necessary evil. Chapter 5 challenges that perception by reimagining performance management as a tool for growth and reflection by asking the important question: Does our current system motivate and empower educators, or does it enforce compliance?

The discussion of MIQs (Most Important Questions) as part of a performance review process represents a profound shift. Instead of focusing solely on what needs to be fixed, this chapter encourages us to consider what is worth growing and where we can help our colleagues develop in ways that inspire their deepest passions. By focusing on the growth of the individual rather than just measuring results, we create a more compassionate, sustainable and effective way to implement performance management.

In schools, as in any workplace, conflict is inevitable. Chapter 6 introduces the concept of 'carefrontation' – approaching difficult conversations with care, honesty and a commitment to maintaining relationships. By using 'carefrontation', leaders set the tone for their teams, creating an environment where tough conversations are not feared, but embraced as opportunities for growth and connection.

Drawing on theories from Kim Scott's book *Radical Candor* and Lisa Nichols' approach to courageous conversations, this chapter provides practical tools to navigate conflict while preserving the integrity of relationships. The chapter calls upon us to recognise that avoiding confrontation encourages problems to fester. The concept of 'carefrontation' emerges as a vital tool for resolving conflict through empathy, clarity and courage. By adopting this approach, leaders ensure that difficult conversations are not destructive but instead offer opportunities to grow, connect and build deeper relationships.

As school leaders, headteachers bear the weight of responsibility for both staff and pupils. Chapter 7 emphasises the importance of self-care. Leaders will find practical advice for creating time for themselves amid the demands of the role. It is not about being a superhero, but about being human and leading from a place of clarity and care. The book, as a whole, also advocates for structural changes in how schools support their leaders, calling for wellbeing support to become a statutory requirement, not an afterthought.

In 'Final Reflections', the culmination of this book's themes is understanding that leadership is not just about leading others, but about a continual evolution of creating a caring culture in which self-care is essential. It is also about being vulnerable enough to know our own needs, brave enough to set boundaries and humble enough to learn alongside our teams. The tools and frameworks presented in this book – whether the transformative power of connecting questions or the reinvention of performance management – are designed to help leaders connect with their teams on a deeper level, creating a culture of trust and mutual respect.

Foreword

This journey through leadership is one that is both personal and professional. As you read each chapter, Shaheen invites you to take the time to reflect on how the strategies and practices she advocates might change your own leadership style and promote self-care. This is more than a book. It is an invitation to join a quiet revolution in how we lead, care, and show up for ourselves and our schools.

Steve Waters and Suneta Bagri, Co-Founders of Teach Well Toolkit

Acknowledgements

With Thanks

My deepest thanks to the contributors who generously shared their words, reflections, and lived experience. Your voices bring depth, honesty, and humanity to these pages, and I am truly grateful for your trust and your courage. To every school leader for trusting me to work with them and their teams. And to you all for reading this book and for leading with humanity.

1
Story of origin – my why

I often start my work on culture, care and connection by asking a simple question:

What is your story of origin?

In other words: What has it taken for you to get here today?

There is a richness to this question. An invitation to step back for a moment or two. Recalling your journey, your trials and tribulations, your key turning points. What it's taken for you to get from there to here. I want to know you; I want to know your why; I want to share, relate, resonate, celebrate, even cry with you. Put simply, I want to connect with you. Knowing your story of origin offers a glimpse into your life, struggles, motivations, dreams and hopes. I gain an insight into who you are on a much deeper level than simply an acquaintance.

So, the paradox here is an interesting one. A deep desire to connect with your 'why' but seldom sharing mine over the 24 years of my career in education. A 'cards close to your chest' type mentality built into my psyche from a young age but particularly the profession of education I entered and namely leadership. We must be the mantras 'Keep it together', 'Show no vulnerability', 'Lead with no signs of weakness'. Of course, this isn't evidenced anywhere nor explicitly taught to us during our early years of leadership. We simply learn by observing others and thus keeping the expectations of minimal vulnerability alive. And the irony is that we frequently ask our children to be emotionally articulate and vulnerable. To somehow open up emotionally and be emotionally available to us at any given time.

So, let's take the opportunity for dialogue now and ask: What is your story of origin?

If I were sat with you in a coaching session, I will have heard your answer to this question by now with no interruptions; I will have given you generative attention, getting lost in your journey, building the picture of you over the chapters of your life. There will or may be twists and turns. The key turning points that define or have defined you, by chance or intentional. I will have built equality and ease into our conversation so that you feel empowered to share your story.

My story of origin

I would like to say that I had my career path set out from a young age. That I had the conditions growing up for success and the environment to support my academic and personal achievements. I often ask others 'What has it taken for you to get from there to where you are now?' Well, in short, it has taken me adversity to get from my starting point to where I am today. That adversity though is my greatest strength; it has illuminated the path before me. It is my why. I remember vividly one key defining moment in time. Mine was during my year 11 exams. A time that, yes, is fraught with revision and exam stress, but I didn't feel any of that. No revision and certainly no stress. I vividly remember the school hall where exams took place, where my key defining moment in life occurred. I was sitting a science exam, again no revision and no stress. I turned every page of that exam paper knowing that I was unable to answer any of the questions. Not because I couldn't read or had special educational needs. I simply couldn't answer the questions because I had no knowledge. I hadn't acquired the necessary knowledge in high school because I seldom attended. I didn't have the luxury to build a schema built on previous knowledge and connecting understanding across curricula. So, I did what I did best at that time of my life. I communicated with the only language I knew: pain. For this I had all the knowledge required and

Story of origin – my why

acquired. I tore my exam paper into small pieces, then sat back in my chair and smiled defiantly.

The key defining moment in time was my permanent exclusion. I would love to have been a fly on the wall when senior leaders decided to permanently exclude me from secondary school. I would have loved to listen in to the conversations that showed no understanding of my context. The lack of attendance (around 30%) as a serious safeguarding concern of need, help and support. No triangulation of evidence over the years on roll. The truancy, the behavior incidents, the risk taking. I was unable to keep myself safe let alone the ones entrusted to. What I needed at that time was unconditional positive regard. I needed the adults to know and understand what I was displaying, what I needed and how to intervene without labelling. I left school without a qualification to my name.

I wouldn't change what happened. I have used the exclusion I faced in every aspect as a child to be as inclusive as I can be as an adult. I used the pain eventually from around 17 years of age to create an intentional life as a catalyst for change, starting my education again and entering the teaching profession. Fast forward 20 years, and I can say how proud I was working for a large city as Deputy Director for Learning within an outstanding Children's Services accountable for the welfare and education of over 118,000 children and young people with zero permanent exclusions. The year I left this post we injected millions of pounds on a model I created for children and young people at serious risk of exclusion by wrapping unconditional regard around them in the form of education inclusion mentors and training the city of schools to detach the labels we consciously and unconsciously place on our most vulnerable.

Yes, I have skipped all the years in between but I have consciously stuck to my key defining moment in time. My 'why' is to create a strong sense of belonging in every school environment for staff and children. Where no one must shed layers of their identity on their way to school or work. Where each environment screams psychological safety. A place where you are welcomed for who you are, what you are, how you are and who you are yet to become. A place of unconditional positive

The Human Side of School Leadership

regard. Where unleashing potential in everyone is the mantra and bias of oppression and micro aggressions conscious in awareness. A place where one of the most beautiful quotes by the eminent coach and author Nancy Kline (1991, 1920) I have heard about inclusion is the fabric of its identity: 'Welcome, and please be the most you, *you* can be. Think as you, act as you, it is you we need.' Imagine such a place exists, where culture, care and connection are infectious and the language everyone uses to communicate is not one of pain but one of acceptance and regard. I exist for this very reason.

I had to walk my path of pain, abuse and disregard to fight for those who can't. As education activist Malala Yousafzai suggests in a powerful speech to the United Nations in 2013: 'I raise up my voice, not to shout but so that those without a voice can be heard. We cannot succeed when half of us are held back.' But don't be fooled, I am an outlier. I am not a story of resilience and grit; I am an outlier. The odds stacked against me as a female British Pakistani raised in a single parent family on free school meals who broke through the prevalence of covert and overt exclusions. I am not the general rule. For every single success story there are countless children failed by the system meant to protect them. In 2022, 20,000 children under the age of six were suspended from schools in the UK. Some 98% of these children struggle in a system of constant exclusions to achieve level 4 or above. Many do not make it out of the collection of failures loaded upon them (Chance UK).

I entered the profession to genuinely make a difference, and my story is only now being shared. A story I am told after each keynote is inspiring and while I want to know that I can inspire what I truly want to do is transform. Transform the way we create care, culture and connection within the workplace to raise positive states of being so that all benefit. My journey started mainly working with children before leading teams and then onto large-scale system leadership. At the heart of this I have held strong and firm a few principles that I have heard countless times echoed back in various forms and guises. The principles in the latter part of my career as a system leader dedicated to removing exclusion in any form through the simplicity of aligning my behaviors and leadership style to be 'better for, not better than' and through the

Story of origin – my why

simple question 'Who does this include and who does this exclude?' along with the tried and tested 'without fear and favour'. Perspective blindness is dangerous, as explored in Matthew Syed's book *Rebel ideas* (2019). Perspective blindness and a lack of lived experience means we close ourselves off from the reality often faced by those we serve. We exclude when we don't understand, when we don't empathise and when we don't look behind the behaviours we deem unacceptable.

The alarming figure of suspensions referenced earlier is a consequence of many complex factors such as lack of funding for SEND (Special Educational Needs and Disabilities), lack of provision, recruitment and retention crisis, Ofsted (the Office for Standards in Education, Children's Services and Skills) pressure to name a few. One aspect of focus for me is creating a haven for staff and children despite the unsurmountable pressures. A haven dripping in care, culture and connection. Why? Because our children and colleagues deserve to feel joy within their learning and work. Because we know that connectedness is a key component for happiness at work. We know that raising the wellbeing of the profession directly impacts on the wellbeing of children.

I left my role as Deputy Director within Children's Services in summer 2023. A role I would most likely have remained in if another key defining moment hadn't occurred in my life. My life path went in a very different direction but never faltering from education, impact and transformation. Education is part of my DNA, as it was for my husband Rhys Myers. We shared our advocacy for education; we shared a deep passion for fighting injustice, fighting for children to be seen and heard. Rhys was the teacher every child wanted; he had a natural affinity for children. Giving them such regard that they unfurled under his care. Often handed the 'hard to reach', he built them up again without the need for words but by his sheer presence. He embodied unconditional positive regard. I would often say that his superpower was reaching the vulnerable, the misrepresented, the judged and given up on with his regard for them as equals, deserving of regard and attention. He is one teacher that no one will ever forget, holding a special place in the hearts of hundreds of children, parents and teachers. He adored the children, his profession and his family. He was an angel walking this earth and

The Human Side of School Leadership

so it was the most shattering experience of my life when I lost my husband tragically and unexpectedly.

I am writing these words from a place of healing because of his regard, care and love. It was so easy to be in a place of communicating through pain all those years ago during high school, but this required healing through the communication of love, radical acceptance and honoring the truly remarkable person he was and who we had the privilege to know and love. When someone so profound causes ripples in what it means to be selfless dies, a part of you dies too. I could sink or honour his memory and everything he stood for. He was my first and only example of pure unconditional positive regard. I had the privilege of being his wife for a short period of our lives, but he remains part of my core for an eternity. Grief is the price we pay for love, as is said.

I wanted to channel my grief into keeping his memory alive and so Balance:ed was born through my second year of grief. At the time, a media storm was brewing around the death of headteacher Ruth Perry. The tragedy of the fragility and fallibility of our leaders when faced with high stakes accountability system. No one should be lost doing the job they love for those who matter the most. I often cite in my keynotes with a very heavy heart the six coroner reports where Ofsted has been cited according to the unions. No one should ever feel that all hope is lost. This only fueled my purpose and mission: to give the leaders unconditional positive regard, create a culture of connection and provide psychological safety.

There are 12 stages of friendship in the Arabic culture. The sixth is Sahib, meaning a friend who is only concerned for your wellbeing. Balance:ed is Sahib, that friend who provides wellbeing supervision for school leaders and staff. A preventative level of safety against the stressors and strains and sometimes perils of the job. Leaders are tasked with creating, governing and being the wellbeing for everyone. Ironically, they have little in terms of their own. Everything to everyone comes to mind for most leaders. Stemming the recruitment crisis, reducing stress-related illnesses, thinking differently about how we connect, using wellbeing to drive performance management and explicitly setting out how we want to be treated is what Balance:ed aims to achieve.

Story of origin – my why

But, above all, the mission of Balance:ed is for leaders to be seen, heard, understood, regarded positively, find our joy, efficacy and reduce suicide rates.

I launched Balance:ed September 2023. It was an easy decision for me. Probably one of the easiest decisions I have made. I intentionally decided not to question it but instead to go with the force that was driving me, propelling me towards this new direction. The natural nervousness, doubt and imposter syndrome did not take hold because I knew in my gut this was the right thing to do. Did I have a clue where to start? No. Had I any experience of starting my own company? No. But despite the lack of experience and even where to start, I did. Small pieces fitting together such as the name of the company popping into my head during a reiki session. Reaching out to a friend to discuss website design when I didn't know where to start. I can't say that I wasn't daunted. I was leaving a secure job for the complete unknown. Complete financial uncertainty. However, the catalyst for my why had now shifted. I wanted to support the profession both Rhys and I adored. Support the retention of our leaders to stay in one of the most rewarding professions despite the significant challenges. To give back using my expertise, experience and regard for everyone working in education. And to work in legacy of my late husband.

So, what exactly was the offer of Balance:ed going to be? After all, my leadership journey was system-wide leadership, large strategic change and influence. What would Balance:ed stand for? The core mission was not difficult to define. I have always been impassioned about wrapping support around leaders who are seldom given the type of support they work so hard to provide for the rest of their staff. Ofsted often asks staff how their wellbeing is supported; this is an indirect question about the school's leadership yet seldom is the same question asked of leaders. Who supports your wellbeing? Leaders report that the Chair of Governors is often a source of support or Chair of the Trust board but often they are not as open and transparent about their wellbeing by virtue of line management within these roles. I hadn't heard of the notion of supervision for wellbeing; for safeguarding, yes, but not for wellbeing. A safe place to share challenges, worries, issues that keep you awake at night. A place of independent, objective and non-judgement space to listen and support with the only aim being the wellbeing of the person in front of you.

Wellbeing supervision is having invaluable time to think, to gather thoughts, to assess, take stock and work through the challenging dynamics of school leadership. I often say that as a leader you are everything to everyone and yet fail to have the same dedicated support for yourself. So why is something so vital in supporting the retention and wellbeing of our leaders so scarcely available? Why is there a lack of commitment? Well, our leaders have simply been given the rhetoric to 'get on with it'. Somehow having wellbeing supervision is a luxury or implies something is wrong. There is often stigma attached to showing vulnerability in education. As mentioned in the first few paragraphs we must remain cool, calm and collected. We are relied upon to have the answers, solutions and must lead by example. The example is 'keep calm and carry on', but at what cost. The body keeps the score and often leaders find themselves recovering from illnesses during mid-term breaks. Sleep deprivation is often cited by leaders, waking at 2am as though an internal alarm clock has sounded but this is exactly what it is. An internal alarm clock, indicating that body and mind cannot rest until the mind and body have had some release. Time to digest and soothe a dysregulated nervous system whether leaders are aware of it or not.

And so, the journey of self-employment began. I was fortunate to be invited into a couple of schools to begin with supporting leaders on their journey of wellbeing mainly through supervision. It was after my first session with three school leaders that I came away without any shadow of doubt that I was doing the right thing. I wanted not only to provide time to think, to share, to evaluate, to offload, but for leaders to feel lighter, understood, safe and completely normal. Using my experience of resonation I quickly developed a professional bond, curtesy and unconditional regard for every school leader I have worked with. I will use a couple of case studies in this book to illustrate the power of supervision for wellbeing and support on elevating a culture of care and connection to raise wellbeing.

Story of origin – my why

My hope is that wellbeing support becomes a statutory offer. We have regulation for preventing and identifying harm for children, and rightly so. The UK Government's Keeping Children Safe in Education initiative is a part of this regulation and mandatory guidance. I feel that we also need 'keeping colleagues safe in education' too. Taking care of our hearts and minds to take care of the young hearts and minds we have been entrusted with. Setting professional standards for wellbeing as a core offer for all staff and in particular leaders will reap dividends. Dedication to preventative and systemic support instead of reactive care often too late when stress is cited for work-related absences.

Your why

I may not know the reasons why you chose this book. I am assuming it's because of your care for human-centered leadership, unconditional regard and how to embed connection without adding to workload a reason for stress-induced absences. Maybe it's for a different perspective on raising and enhancing wellbeing. I would love to know your why; I would love to connect with you. Please feel free to reach out to me on info@balance-ed.co.uk.

How to use this book

Now, please bear with me. I am most certainly not telling you how to suck eggs. But what I *do* want to give is a sense of how I want to gift this book to you. How I want you to experience this book. I want this to be a conversation, a dialogue, not a monologue. I want to provoke thinking by asking questions you have most likely never been asked in education. I want you to feel inspired, motivated, as though you have voice, influence and efficacy. I want to offer you a practical guide to creating a culture of wellness in your setting by virtue of connectedness and not an add-on or in addition to, thus defeating the point of the book. The chapters will offer questions, reflections, case studies and opportunities to connect with me. You can dip into chapters, of course, but to fully appreciate the aims of the book I would recommend reading each chapter in order.

I am offering something tangible and tactical with this guide. A tried and tested way of connecting to deepen and strengthen existing relationships. I am offering my experience over my time in education, my story of origin and the adversity, my experience working as a founder of Balance:ed. I am also offering my pain of losing someone who made a profound difference in education so that children felt they mattered the most and came to believe that they did. It takes a special person to create a wonderous environment of unconditional regard. It takes special people to create a strong sense of belonging so that children want to come to school and staff love coming to work. I often say that we don't need to enforce an attendance policy if our sense of belonging is strong. We owe our profession the personal care and attention we give others so readily. Educationalists are unique in their relentless pursuit to improve outcomes in whatever matrix you wish to define this. I often say that education is running on the goodwill of so many dedicated individuals, who at best should be proud of what they achieve for the benefit of others.

> **Connecting questions**
>
> You will find connecting questions at the start of each chapter, as you did within this chapter:
> *What is your story of origin?*
> *What has it taken for you to get from there to where you are today?*
> *What are your key defining moments that have shaped your path and who you are, positive or negative?*

Chapter summary

This first chapter sets the tone for the entire book. It's not a manual, a checklist, nor a leadership toolkit; it's a conversation. We open

Story of origin – my why

with the truth about the weight that leaders carry, the way our titles can slowly swallow the people we are, and how we often measure ourselves by impossible standards. We explore the tension between vulnerability and professionalism, the push and pull of wanting to be open yet fearing it may be seen as weakness.

I share candid reflections on the realities of school leadership: the loneliness, the responsibility and the silent pressure to 'hold it all together' while never letting the cracks show. I question the models of leadership that have been passed down to us and whether they truly serve us or if they simply teach us to perform at the cost of our wellbeing.

Throughout, there's an undercurrent of invitation: to strip back the roles and titles, to reconnect with the human being at the centre, and to consider what it would be like to lead without guilt, without the relentless striving for perfection. This chapter reminds us that leadership is not about being flawless; it's about being present, aware and grounded enough to make decisions that honour both people and purpose.

Interludes

From this chapter onwards, this book will include 'Interludes' – communications from leaders across education who have generously shared a quote that resonates deeply with them and the story behind their choice. These moments will give us a glimpse into the person behind the role, the experiences that have shaped them and the values they carry into their leadership. Getting to know leaders beneath their roles is not a luxury; it's how trust is built, how connection deepens and how we remember that no one leads in isolation. It also reveals their story of origin, their key defining moments, how they lead and what they believe in and about themselves and others.

Interlude 1
by Ann Palmer

> The following perspective sits at the heart of what Ann Palmer, CEO of Fig Tree International and executive coach, shares in her reflection: 'A leader who tends the roots of culture, waters the soul with well-being, and shelters hearts with contentment, will find people standing tall, blooming with strength and grace.'

Ann's reflection

This quote encapsulates a profound truth about the relational and holistic nature of leadership. It suggests that effective leadership is not simply about direction, control or strategic vision, but about cultivating the conditions in which individuals and communities can thrive. In particular, it emphasises the interconnectedness of culture, wellbeing and contentment as the foundational roots from which strong and resilient organisations emerge.

The metaphor of 'tending the roots' positions leadership as an act of cultivation rather than domination. Leadership is often imagined as a top-down exertion of authority, but here it is framed as a process of stewardship and nurture. Culture, in this sense, represents the soil in which organisational life is planted. Research consistently demonstrates that culture shapes behaviours, values and relationships within institutions, and leaders who attend carefully to culture can profoundly influence collective identity and purpose (Schein, 2017). By tending culture, leaders ensure that norms of respect, equity, and belonging are embedded, enabling all members of the community to flourish.

The phrase 'waters the soul with well-being' foregrounds the moral responsibility of leaders to safeguard the health and vitality of those they serve. In contemporary debates on leadership, the concept of wellbeing has emerged as a central concern, particularly in sectors such as education, healthcare and social work, where emotional and physical exhaustion are prevalent. The imagery of watering the soul implies that wellbeing is not an ancillary concern but a life-giving necessity. Leaders who ignore wellbeing risk creating environments of burnout, disengagement and attrition. Conversely, leaders who intentionally create structures and practices that promote balance, psychological safety and fulfilment generate the conditions for long-term sustainability and productivity (Harter et al., 2020).

The third dimension of the quote, 'shelters hearts with contentment', invites reflection on the concept of contentment as distinct from mere happiness. Contentment suggests a state of inner peace, security and acceptance that comes from knowing one's contribution is valued and one's identity affirmed. Leadership through contentment does not mean suppressing ambition or growth but creating a climate in which individuals do not feel constantly threatened, judged or compared. This aligns with the ethics of care (Gilligan, 1982), which emphasises attentiveness, responsibility and responsiveness to the needs of others. Leaders who embody this ethic build trust and loyalty, establishing environments where people feel both protected and empowered.

The culmination of the metaphor 'people standing tall, blooming with strength and grace' suggests that the ultimate outcome of leadership grounded in culture, wellbeing and contentment is not compliance or performance for its own sake, but the flourishing of human dignity and potential. Leadership becomes transformative when it elevates individuals beyond survival into spaces of growth, creativity and resilience. This vision resonates with theories of servant leadership (Greenleaf, 1977), where the leader's primary role is to serve others, enabling their growth and with transformational leadership (Bass, 1990), which inspires collective purpose and moral uplift.

From an applied perspective, the quote challenges leaders to reframe their priorities. It suggests that cultivating culture, safeguarding wellbeing and nurturing contentment are not 'soft' or secondary dimensions of leadership but rather core strategic imperatives. A school leader, for example, who focuses solely on examination results or accountability metrics without tending to the wellbeing and cultural belonging of staff and students risks creating a toxic environment in which performance is unsustainable. By contrast, a leader who fosters inclusive culture prioritises rest and renewal, and models contentment, can achieve sustainable excellence while preserving human dignity. Moreover, the quote implicitly critiques leadership models that privilege speed, efficiency or individual achievement over community flourishing. It affirms the necessity of slowing down, listening deeply and recognising that true growth comes from invisible but

The Human Side of School Leadership

vital processes beneath the surface the cultivation of roots rather than the decoration of branches.

Finally, the imagery of roots, water and shelter carries a spiritual resonance. It evokes traditions of stewardship, care and covenant found in many religious and philosophical traditions. By grounding leadership in relational care and moral responsibility, the quote gestures towards a vision of leadership as an ethical vocation rather than a functional role.

The quote invites leaders to reconsider what it means to lead well. It challenges dominant narratives of leadership that equate success with power, visibility or control, instead proposing a vision rooted in culture, wellbeing and contentment. Such leadership, attentive to the invisible yet essential dimensions of human flourishing, ensures that individuals and communities not only survive but 'stand tall, blooming with strength and grace'.

Ultimately, the quote reminds us that leadership is not a performance but a practice of care, an art of tending the unseen roots so that life above ground may flourish with dignity, resilience and beauty.

2
Care, connection and culture

> **Connecting question:** Are people connected to you because of your title or because of who you are?

The connecting question above serves well to stimulate conversation, a question that goes beyond the superficial. It is to provoke thought and reflection. The more senior the position the more relevant this question is. Take a moment to reflect on this question: Do people know you because of *who* you are or because of *what* you are – headteacher, CEO, deputy headteacher and so on? It asks us to move from the distinguishable leadership styles and types to who we are as individuals. Of course, our styles can be determined by our value set, which is determined by our personality and so forth, but it asks whether people feel connected to who we are rather than what we are (the title). In other words, do we make it easy for people to describe who we are as opposed to what we do? An interesting concept given that we spend a large proportion of our time at work interacting with colleagues and yet seldom spend time on defining connection with others.

Who we are beneath the titles

My keynote presentations focus on care, connection and culture – one of my most requested themes. We love the thought of understanding the components of connection and culture. Having affirmation without sometimes using the word 'wellbeing' does help. We want to know we're doing a good job, seeking affirmation and validation. What does care, culture and connection look like? Well, first, the three components are interrelated. To *care* we are setting placement for *culture* and for both *care* and *culture* to exist we need *connection*. What sets apart thriving schools and trusts is the intentionality of all three components. Sometimes we believe that setting a policy for wellbeing actively creates and contributes to a healthy culture; after all, we are cementing the notion and vision on paper for everyone to see. If we are lucky, we invite stakeholders to contribute to its development rolling out what we believe wellbeing to mean in our workplace. Often the mental health lead or wellbeing lead is assigned the task of creating a policy. The irony is that the individuals in our organisations are the ones who wear many hats and have very little training on what wellbeing truly means to create a strong sense of care, culture and connection.

Wellbeing exists in all manner of aspects within our workplace. It is rooted in culture, in our schools our trusts vision, within our trust strategic plan and school development plans; it is inextricably linked to our school evaluation form (SEF). It is felt during lunchtimes, in the school hall, staffroom and within the corridors. It is within the very fabric of the ecosystem that is 'school' and yet we place emphasis that wellbeing is what we do for staff as opposed to how are we as a 'staff'. Shifting the interpretation of wellbeing from something we 'do' to something we 'are' takes the pressure out of creating a tickbox exercise of 'things' we do to support the wellbeing of our staff.

The subtle shift from 'doing' wellbeing to 'being' well

We have somehow become confused with what wellbeing truly means, believing it to be something that can be addressed by the amount and what we offer (perks), including a reduction in workload. We see it as experiences to offer as opposed to feelings we can create. Raising positive states of being is wellbeing. Feeding culture, care and connection as something tangible and tactical surrounded in relational practice elevates positive states of being and is wellbeing. Being well means we find joy and satisfaction in our work, we have high resilience against

Care, connection and culture

challenges, we embrace growth. Our positive to negative ratio can often be high. Our positive to negative talk can often be high. This does not mean we are positive all the time, a term described as 'toxic positivity'; it means that we are intentional in how we act and feel. Intention and the right environment steeped in care, culture and connection means we can move from surviving to thriving.

So how do we elevate positive states of being. According to the Teacher Wellbeing Index (2023), 95% of headteachers have felt the highest levels of stress ever reported, with 89% of senior leaders feeling the same. We can often blame the demands of the role, changing Department for Education (DfE) goalposts, a looming Ofsted or recent poor inspection, workload, challenging behaviour, parental complaints – the list goes on. I often say that education is, and has been a for a while, running on the good will of people. Where common sense prevails, and people just get stuck into whatever improvements they can make, going above and beyond. But at what cost? The body and mind keeps a score, with sleepless nights or disturbed sleep being one of the indicators of high stress toll. I often start my coaching asking, 'What keeps you awake at night?' and then it all comes tumbling out after a few minutes of tossing and turning around the mind of solutions, problems, challenges, etc.

I am going to take you through my keynote on care culture and connection in this chapter, to illustrate, highlight and provoke what we already know as wellbeing but have made complicated by defining a policy for it based on the 'offer'. Nothing will come as a surprise to you, but it will deepen your awareness of how care, culture and connection can be embedded so easily. *Tangible and tactical* is my tag line. Yes, I want to inspire you but mostly I want to transform practice by providing the questions and mode to elevate positive states of being. To help take care of our colleagues' hearts and minds so that they can take care of the young hearts and minds.

According to Jay Shetty in *Think Like a Monk*, Buddhist monks say there are three cancers of the mind – comparing, criticising and complaining. Now I know that we all find ourselves in one of these and possibly all three from time to if you have mastered them well enough (tongue in cheek). The cancers are described as taking hold and spreading to all areas of our life, our perspectives, the lens we view things with and how we interpret events and interact with others. The three cancers actively lower positive states of being. We can, according to how often we engage in the three Cs, become stuck physically and emotionally without realising it. When I mention this during keynotes audience members normally pictures someone who complains incessantly; it is surprising how quickly we can identify people who lower culture often unintentionally. There is one antidote however, and it also begins with the letter C: *connectedness*. It is scientifically proven that the quality of life is determined by the people we spend most of our time with. Relationships matter more than we think, including relationships at work, and connectedness is at the heart of how well we relate to one another.

Belonging as the backbone of performance

According to the Harvard professor Arthur C. Brooks (2023), who is also known as the world's 'happiness expert', negativity is an emotional contagion. It is easily spread from person to person, room to room, leaving remnants in its wake. You can see how infectious complaining, criticising and comparing is. Interact with one negative emotion or person and you're holding the same emotion without sometimes realising it. Arthur C. Brooks has written over 13 books that research culture and happiness. Positivity is a tool mastered. It is not negating reality or challenges, but it is also an emotional contagion, just a positive one, that can be felt, heard and seen once you step into a school. The very first interactions you have demonstrate the power of positivity or challenges of negativity.

Owen Eastwood (the world's most in demand performance coach), in his book *Belonging* (2021), discusses the concept of creating a strong sense of belonging and identity, and how this maximises performance. He outlines how the Māori culture use the term 'Whakapapa', which means belonging and identity. At the core is responsibility for the wellbeing and individual identity of its people. It screams 'you belong and how you feel matters'. Intentionally wanting to know you on a deeper

Care, connection and culture

level is what is considered to bring pride, joy, satisfaction and peak performance in many of the accolades achieved by Māori sportspeople. Eastwood goes on to describe the sporting organisations in which culture is strong, resulting in a single indicator of the sporting stars' and teams' successes (and vice versa when it isn't).

I use connecting questions to provoke thinking around strength of connectedness at work, stimulating thought around whether we believe connectedness is stronger than it is. One question I ask is: 'Do you know the prevalence of loneliness in your organisation?' This is the opposite of connectedness. It's seldom asked on staff surveys but is a good question to understand the prevalence, if there is any. After all, we will have colleagues who spend most of their time in a classroom or office with little contact with their peers during the school day and sometimes little contact with significant others at home. I have been told that the staffroom is seldom visited anymore in many schools. Staff busy preparing for the afternoon lessons or marking. Sometimes the only 'togetherness' is during staff meetings or INSET (In-service Education and Training days).

Turning existing practices into catalysts for change

So how do we begin to build care, culture and connection? How do we take care of hearts and minds within such a busy work environment with so many competing demands. We tend to, without any fault of our own, work through so many statutory compliant responsibilities while upholding the whole school system in its entirety and therefore the role of wellbeing falls to an individual or a couple of individuals wearing additional hats and little time. Throw in some wellbeing mental health accredited training and one policy later and, *ta-da*, we have wellbeing sorted. Sometimes we haven't the time to consider what we already have in place to aid wellbeing. I talk about tangible and tactical. No add-ons or additions to but rather what is within our existing structure. Wellbeing is not separate from the day to day. It sometimes can't be measured by what we think we must offer.

The Human Side of School Leadership

To elevate positive states of being we use what is at our disposable. It is in the everyday, every interaction, staff meeting, CPD (continuing professional development), INSET, whatever you want to call it. These existing structures are the perfect place to intentionally create connectedness and elevate positive states of being. Once we understand that creating the interactions we have reminds us and others of our mission, vision and values, we can start to intentionally create meaningful discussions.

Intentionally creating space for relational practice to strengthen and grow is the place to start. Relationships matter more than we think and often can be the direct link between happiness and dissatisfaction at work. In the Harvard Business Series on Emotional Intelligence, Gretchen Spreitzer and Christine Porath (2012) outline the importance of relational practice. They mention investing in relationships that energise you. We may have colleagues who are great but difficult to work with and, as mentioned earlier, negativity is an emotional contagion and their mode of operating. Spreitzer and Porath go on to say that individuals who thrive look for opportunities to work closely with colleagues who energise us and minimise those who drain our energy. Whenever I discuss the 'three cancers of the mind' during my keynote speech I often have headteachers say that they can picture the person/s to whom this applies and how they drain the energy and efforts of the school.

So how do we encourage our colleagues to thrive and elevate positive states of being using our existing structures as we have defined earlier. We start by seeking to build good relationships through every meeting and interaction with connection. We intentionally create space to connect beyond the superficial check-in questions we may have had experience with such as: 'What tv show are you watching at the moment?' When we intentionally create space for connection, we create space for psychological safety to grow. You see, psychological safety is not in the absence of threat but in the presence of connection. Psychological safety elevates positive states of being. It allows colleagues to be seen, heard and valued. It creates a strong sense of identity and belonging.

Care, connection and culture

Individuality is embraced, diversity of thought is valued and you feel like you matter.

Using connecting questions at the start of meetings is one way to strengthen relationships. When working with teams to build cohesiveness and understanding of each other I often start with: 'What has taken you to get from where you were to where you are now?' Very similar to the question around story of origin.

> **Reflection exercise**
>
> So let me ask *you*: 'What has it taken you to get from where you were to where you are today?' Spend some time on this question. Gather your thoughts, write down what comes to mind, celebrate your wins and tribulations because it all builds to who you are today.
>
> If I was presented with this question, I would say that is has taken me enormous strength and resilience to face and rise from challenges both personally and professionally. I would mention my permanent exclusion, my turbulent childhood, entering education with no starting point, having a young family while studying for my degree and learning, divorce, grief, starting a new business and so on. I would mention a couple of those to spark curiosity from colleagues. To let them see me beneath my role. In the words, using my vulnerabilities as something to engage curiosity rather than rejection.

Connection as the gateway to psychological safety

In most cases all we need is one excellent connecting question at the start of the meeting. I encourage leaders to present the question prior to the meeting because people want time to absorb and process; after all, we want to deepen psychological safety. Time to think is one of the most valuable commodities we have yet are seldom able to engage with in the 'businesses of the role'. We intentionally create 'time to think' within our meetings so that the answers are meaningful, rich and inviting for us to share. We create the time to connect because we know that relationships matter more than we think, and the quality of thinking and feeling in our school is related to this, to the strength of connection.

Connecting questions do just that. They give us the opportunity to share with one another in safety and acceptance. You may wish to set up the psychological safety principles when sharing personal information, but it must feel authentic in its nature. Of course, people do not have to answer a question and respectfully we allow space for this, but often people do feel comfortable and confident to share over time. I will go into more depth and include practical details to embed intentional connection in Chapter 4.

What we are creating is care, culture and connection intentionally using what exists at our fingertips. We start with one aspect until the quality of that spills into all other areas. Everything will improve when the quality of relationships and thinking improves. Running meetings (staff and others) in a way that fosters and cultivates care is a sure-fire winner. I often hear from staff during my wellbeing audits that they miss the level of chat during meetings, which are now mainly based on CPD. They miss and crave for the connection and opportunity to talk with one another. Sometimes it's remembering to connect before content. Reminding ourselves that we are in the business of people and children, and that connecting before content is taught sets the environment for learning and being. Consideration for colleagues who may only converse with pupils on a day-to-day basis could in fact be quite lonely and isolating, coming back full circle to my question: 'Do we know the prevalence of loneliness within our school/academy/trust?'

Care, connection and culture

Why staff surveys only scratch the surface

This leads me onto staff surveys. In essence they serve as a tool to capture staff morale, motivation, aptitude, culture, efficacy and so on. Often, we know the results before we have asked the questions. I question staff surveys for the purpose they fulfill. Do the surveys have the type and quality of questions that allow us to measure the culture and care of the organistion? Do they truly capture the day-to-day motivation, stressors and desires of staff? They have a place in offering a sounding board anonymously, but in conservations with leaders and staff over the years I can honestly say that the answers are in what is *not* said. Staff can feel that the tickbox-exercise staff surveys are not a true reflection of their current reality and often miss the opportunity to capture what really motivates them, nor is the individuality of the person represented. We often expect leaders to take the trends, patterns and action in a 'you said, we did' format, seldom realising the subtle nuances that staff and leaders may share concerns and do not wish for those to lead on their feedback ironically. Leaders tasked with main responsibility for improving actions from the surveys further sets the divide. Surely a more holistic and independent approach ensures that all staff feel supported in interpreting and actioning what the survey may suggest needs to be approached as well as celebrating the wins.

Audits are a great measure of culture, care and connection. Types of questions that I ask staff are made to extrapolate the determiners of cause and effect. To paint a true picture of thought and feelings. Having someone who has been in the role and understands the external pressures also helps. Having run several audits, I am always struck by how open and honest staff are. Of course the principles of safety are always set up, but telling staff that their voice and influence is valued sets the tone for the audit. People need to feel efficacy and, most importantly, self-efficacy. The platform to have a voice and to influence change is an intrinsic motivation and correlates with feelings of hope. The Co-operative Group runs a wellbeing index for communities. A low wellbeing score can often be linked to low self-efficacy: 'What is the point when my voice isn't heard or I can't influence the experience by which I live and am governed by?'

One question that I use to determine staff feeling quickly is from the question: 'Have you felt like leaving the profession?' I then go on to ask how recent the feeling has been and whether they feel they can be open about the reasons. I'm drawing out the reasons which they often share whether the word 'why' is there or not. This is a powerful question. When asked independently of the school or multi-academy trust, it is a good indicator of the current culture of the school or external pressures. What the question implies to staff from the outset of the audit is this: 'Your opinion, your voice, your feelings and your motivation matter, and I understand the pressures and demands you are facing.' Creating a true space of feedback is what elevates positive states of being regardless of the answers.

Another powerful question I ask both to children and staff is: 'What does your headteacher/teacher value?' Together, these two questions provide 90% of the strength of culture, care and connection. When staff can cite that a leader values care, empathy, high standards, kindness, themselves and so forth, you know that the leader/s embody these values authentically for the benefit of all. When the answers centre around the expectations on them to deliver as a main driver and unrealistic demands, being available and having to 'get on' with it, then you can see what type of culture is, and has been, created. Owen Eastwood, in his book *Belonging* (2021), outlines how the footballer Michael Owen explains that his performance improved and declined as a direct result of how much he felt he belonged in a culture that cared deeply about the team members. Asking children the same question is often eye-opening. Answers range from: 'They care about success but not how I can get there'; 'They want me to tuck my shirt in'; and 'Being quiet'; to 'They care about me and what I think'; 'Kindness, fun and doing well'; and '*Me*: they value *me*, not just my outcomes'. You can see why I started this chapter with the connecting question: 'Are people connected to you because of your title or because of who you are?'

Care, connection and culture

Creating a strong sense of belonging places people first. Leadership styles that are human-centred, that show strength, vulnerability and warmth, are the most preferred by colleagues according to the *Harvard Business Review* on Leadership Presence (2020). Authors Cuddy, Kohut and Neffinger in *Connect, Then Lead* (2013), mention that when we project warmth and authenticity people feel calm, reassured and safe in our presence. They go on to ask the question: 'Do you project warmth?'

In my work with leaders, I often ask them to them to describe who they are beneath their roles? I use 'roles' to mean the many different hats we wear or titles we possess. I often ask the questions that don't appear on NPQs (National Professional Qualifications) or staff surveys. I want to know who you are so that I can connect with you because I've only connected to you because of your title thus far. Often, we have dialogue around this question. It reveals a lot before we get to a core set of values. Answers often go into other roles when what I am prodding at is for you to tell me who you are before and beneath your roles. What are your desires, wishes, values and behaviours? I then go on to ask if we believe that these are demonstrated. I get a 'yes' most of the time. Often there can be a dissonance between what we believe we show and do, and how this is perceived and received. This, everyone, is the real staff survey. In the reflection exercise that follows are a set of questions to determine care, culture and connection as a starting point for us.

The question that changes the conversation

The reflection exercise here is time for us to consider before we embrace the questions as a senior leadership team. Time for you as a leader to benchmark against your perceptions. Answer them often with what first comes to mind. There is no judgement in being your true authentic self.

The Human Side of School Leadership

> **Reflection exercise**
>
> Spend 20–30 minutes on these questions. Have a notebook (or some other means) handy to jot down your answers.
>
> 1. Who am I beneath my roles?
> 2. Have we asked our teams what we value?
> 3. Have we created space for authentic feedback?
> 4. Do we connect before content?
> 5. Have we created space for intentional connection?
> 6. Have we defined what cultures means to me/to us to the school?
>
> The next few chapters define simple yet transformative practices I have used and use within my work on everything care, culture and connection. They are tried and tested as the case studies will outline. One of my favorites is 'Teach me how to treat you'.
>
> Thank you for reading and engaging with the questions posed in this chapter. They are meant to be soul-stirring and thought-provoking. My hope is to stir your thinking back to what drives you within your leadership role, to give you some background into why care, culture and connecting matters but in a straightforward sense. I understand how busy you are, what you may be juggling and how you want to show up to make the difference you set out to make. I stand with you.

Chapter summary

This chapter goes deeper into the idea that leadership is not just about outcomes; it's about presence, connection and the culture we cultivate every single day. We explore the fine line between 'doing' wellbeing and genuinely 'being' well, recognising that staff and leaders alike can feel when the work is a tickbox exercise versus when it's real.

Through personal reflection and real-world examples, I unpick the forces that both erode and strengthen culture. The three Cs that

Care, connection and culture

harm – comparing, complaining and criticising – are contrasted with the one C that heals – connection. And not surface connection, but the kind where people feel known, valued and understood. Because belonging is not a fluffy add-on; it's the core driver of sustainable performance and resilience.

We also challenge assumptions about leadership titles, staff surveys and the invisible gaps in communication that shape morale. Audits are reframed not as judgement tools, but as cultural mirrors, reflecting back the truths we might be missing in the busyness of daily school life.

Throughout, I pose the uncomfortable yet essential question: 'Who are you beneath your role?' It's an invitation to strip back the layers, to remember the person behind the position, and to reconnect with the values and motivations that brought you into leadership in the first place. Because when we do that, the culture changes not through policies alone, but through people showing up differently.

Interlude 2
by Mary Myatt

> 'Stephen Covey (1989) once said: 'When you show deep empathy toward others, their defensive energy goes down, and positive energy replaces it. That's when you can get more creative in solving problems.' This perspective from Mary Myatt (education advisor, author and speaker) sits at the heart of her reflection on this quote.'

Mary's reflection

This quote doesn't mean that everyone is their best friend, but it does mean that thoughtful leaders see the human being beyond the function. Men and women are more than their work. They have a life beyond the confines of the daily nine to five, or whatever. They have the joys and the sadness which are the lot of every human being. While they might be put on hold when at work, they are still there in the background, bubbling away. This background doesn't need to be brought to the table, but it does need to be acknowledged.

There is an excellent example of this in a Birmingham (UK) school. The head is never in his office, because he is out and about. He cares passionately about his school and everyone in it. At the start of the school day, he is at the school gate and often in the street outside, urging students to come in, hurry up, get a move on. That's because he doesn't want them to miss a moment of the good things that are in store for them. He sees them as humans first and students second. He cares about them as individuals, he knows that for many of them life is tough, but he makes no excuses. While they are with him and his colleagues, he makes it clear that he enjoys their company and expects them to do well.

Interlude 2

This is a feature of many top leaders. A combination of warmth and tough love. Another head, a towering personality, exudes a warmth and a critical concern for all those he works with and teaches. He cares about them as human beings first and as professionals second. I once saw this through a window as he spoke to a student. I couldn't hear the conversation but I could see the expression on his face. He addressed the student sternly, asked her a few questions, waited for her response and managed a smile in his eyes. She turned on her heels and headed back to where she was meant to be going. It was a moment of 'extreme' care. And it said, *get cracking with what you are meant to be doing, stop bunking your lesson. You matter and your work matters*. The subtext was: *You are a human being and your success matters to me*.

Teachers do this when they are waiting for their students to arrive. Whether they are standing at the door as they come into the lesson, or are already inside, they convey a warmth which says I am glad you are here, I'm glad you are in my lesson, we are going to be doing some interesting things today. The temperature is different in these places. There is still the liveliness and bustle and boisterousness of a lot of young people making either way around a school, but there is a tangible sense of purpose because everyone knows they matter.

Now the teacher is able to do this because she knows that she matters. She may be lucky enough to have this sense of mattering in her personal life. She also knows that this is a place where she matters. So how does this happen? It is not always put into words, but is more often felt. She knows that her headteacher values her not just for the professional skills she brings to the job but for the individual that she is. How is it possible to pull this off in a large setting? Whether it is large or small, the principles are the same. The tone is set by the leader at the top, who knows that power must be underpinned by authority. And while power comes with the role, authority comes from the consistency and humanity with which a leader goes about his daily business. Everyone matters, and that means *everyone*, including teaching assistants, cleaning staff, lunchtime staff and caretakers. And it goes without saying that the students and parents are included in 'everyone'. There are several things that top leaders do to achieve this. First, they know everyone's names. How is this possible in a setting with more than 1,000 students and adults in it? Well, they make the decision that this is important, so they make it happen. What I have noticed is that the leaders who make the effort to know everyone's names occasionally forget them. This seems not to matter because people realise that they are making the effort.

The Human Side of School Leadership

They know the names not only of all their staff, naturally, but they also make a point of noting something about their personal lives too. They are skilled in knowing the right information to refer to. Things like: 'How did your son's sports trials go?', 'How is your daughter getting on at university?', 'How's the allotment going?', 'Are things ok?'. They are investing in the wider part of the human being, beyond their work. And the impact of this? Everyone knows that they are valued, why would they want not to do their best or work anywhere else? They are being affirmed at the deepest level and it is a deeply satisfying thing to experience.

At a classroom level, teachers invest time either at the beginning of a term or meeting a class for the first time by getting to know their students. This is done, not just to make the running of the classroom smoother but to make a deeper connection with the young people they are working with. They know that the people in front of them are more important than the piece of paper which is their lesson plan. This need not take long, but it signals an attitude about the way we do business here. It says 'You matter, I matter and together we are going to be doing important work.'

The leaders working to the principles of humans first, professionals second are not agony aunts. They are not everyone's best friend. They don't think it is their duty to sort out everyone's problems, but they are saying 'You matter, I appreciate you and I know you will do your best work here.'

What happens is that there is a 'bank balance' of goodwill. And it means that when it needs to be drawn on for tough conversations (there are always tough conversations), the underlining message is that 'You're ok but this aspect of your work needs addressing, so what are we doing to do about it?'

They distinguish the work from the human being. They know that it is possible to be robust but kind. But the kindness always comes first.

3
Teach me how to treat you

> **Connecting question**: How would I want to be encouraged right now?

'How would I want to be encouraged right now?' is a seemingly straightforward question. It asks us to delve into how we want to be treated. It puts us in the driving seat to determine how we want to be encouraged. Asking us to identify the behaviours of encouragement to us and for us. To identify we must ask ourselves what encouragement looks like personally and professionally, often interconnected. You may have come across love languages and, as you may know, there are five of these: words of affirmation, physical touch, acts of service, gift giving and quality time. We determine ours by identifying which language we most resonate with and enjoy receiving. We select how we want to receive love and often assume that others can second guess how we want to be treated because we feel vulnerable sharing what helps us be seen, heard and understood.

Moving beyond values lists

I can't recall being asked the connecting question during an interview or meeting or, in fact, a performance review. I have, though, been given a list of values to adopt in my professional behaviours deemed acceptable, appropriate and to advance the school or trust, but never my individual choices in how I would like to be treated. There certainly isn't room for this in a staff survey. We know that self-efficacy is a powerful determinate of engagement and satisfaction. Have a go at answering the question, if you haven't done so already. What did you identify? There are personal preferences for encouragement and often the leaders I work with who have never been asked the question are expected to know how others would like to be treated. Having a code of conduct and professional behaviours does outline hard boundaries but doesn't consider individuality.

To create a strong sense of belonging and to embed inclusion we encourage individuality. To promote equality and equity we tailor our offer to be as inclusive as possible. Have we ever delved into how staff truly want to be treated at work? What would the outcome be if we opened the opportunity for staff to first think about how they wish to be treated and how to articulate their thoughts. This is not a wish list, however, but a tangible and tactical way of defining what we think works for us. The process itself in identifying how we wish to be treated alone makes us think about motivators and encouragers. We are forced to think about whether we disable or enable others as a byproduct of this.

Conversations that build connection and safety

You may think that this could open a can of worms, and we therefore must treat people in a manner of different ways. Let me reassure you, in the schools I have worked with on 'Teach me how to treat you' we have engaged in rich discussion (creating the bonding hormone oxytocin). Explored what it means to be valued and to have our voice heard (psychological safety). To have the opportunity for and often the first time to really think about how we wish to shape our working relationships (autonomy and self-efficacy).

As leaders we spend most of our time managing relationships. Both positive and negative. People management can and often does take up a large amount of time. We learn how to handle conflict whether confidently or not, but we try. Again, no rulebook but a suite of leaderships styles and experiences to rely on. Thinking differently about people management can often be the first step. For example, I often call the CEO not a Chief Executive Officer but Chief Engagement Officer instead. It puts engagement of the organisation at the core. Each opportunity to engage with colleagues not just manage them against the mission, vision and key performance indicators (KPIs.)

We can see the interplay between Chapter 2's question 'are people connected to you because of your title or because of who you are', here. We all seek validation and affirmation within our roles. We may not need rewards but recognition for hard work and determination helps us to feel trusted and supported. After all, keeping staff within their roles out of desire and motivation should be a key driver.

The science behind positive states of being

So how does 'Teach me how to treat you' work. I first introduced this in the early days of Balance:ed. As I have said before, wellbeing is not an offer but how you feel within the organisation daily. According to Dr Tara Swart on her podcast with Jay Shetty, it's a state of being. Feeling positive creates oxytocin and feeling stressed creates the stress hormone cortisol. The associated feelings with oxytocin are love, trust, joy and excitement as opposed to the correlating feelings with cortisol being shame, sadness, anger, disgust and fear. We want to raise positive states of being and hard wire the brain with positive experiences at work increasing rates of resilience, which, by the way, we have in buckets.

Transforming meetings

With anything introduced into education, everyone always wants a WAGOLL (what a good one looks like). The process versus the outcome is often the most rewarding. This is where growth happens. I facilitate a 'Teach me how to treat you' with senior leaders first. Senior leadership teams work closely with one another to improve outcomes and drive strategy. Meeting once, often twice, a week and daily interactions mean that the quality of thinking is a direct result of the quality of the relationships and therefore the quality of work.

See how I put *quality of thinking* first. I have had the privilege of working with many senior leadership teams and I have yet to find a team who have not interrupted one another. Interruptions stop thinking and without any fault of our own we fall prey to a busy and tight agenda needing quick-fire solutions. I transform meetings into a haven of quality thinking with a carefully curated agenda to promote the finest thinking and elevate positive states of being. Meetings you look forward to as opposed to dreading. Meetings in which your contributions matter and solutions arrive quicker and feel more meaningful.

Do we know what our leadership teams think about meetings? Do we know how they want them to run to get the best thinking and leave the meeting feeling accomplished and heard? Have we asked how long between questions and feedback we give so that there is time for everyone to process what has been heard and asked of them? I will delve into the topic on transforming meetings in the next chapter, but this ties in nicely with 'Teach me how to treat you'. It is purposefully curious.

Small but significant acts of regard

Being curious in understanding how our colleagues want to be treated creates a sense of belonging. We are not expected to carry around with us the differences in how everyone wants to be greeted in the morning like so many teacher morning classroom greetings individualised to every pupil. It's about the way people like to be treated in the big but individual ways. I once had a headteacher tell me in her 'Teach me how to treat you': 'I just want to be asked how I am in the morning.' That's it. She simply asked everyone how they were but never received it back. Everyone assuming that everyone else had asked or the dangerous assumption that the head doesn't have to be asked, or the even more dangerous assumption that the head doesn't need asking because they should be fine. Another head mentioned that she has a busy morning with small children before arriving at school and is unintentionally made to feel guilty for not arriving early.

It's the small things that chip away at us. We assume that a blanket approach of treating everyone as outlined in values and professional behaviours should be enough. We can often feel guilty or embarrassed in airing how we wish to be treated. As though somehow, we are selfish for stating our own needs. But this is the very essence of raising positive states of being. It makes us stop and think – often for the first time – how we wish to be treated and, in turn, how we want to be encouraged. Imagine having that as a question during performance reviews or during an interview. I know it may stop you in your tracks, but having your skillset and knowledge so readily available at your fingertips should be how you as a person wish to be treated professionally. We should not feel ashamed or selfish to define our professional boundaries.

Bringing 'Teach me how to treat you' to education

A 'Teach me how to treat you' is simply an outline of how you would like interactions to be with you. There is no right or wrong. It never existed in the realm of education until its introduction through Balance:ed in October 2023. Working with members of the senior leadership team at the time and finally onto teachers once senior leaders felt comfortable and confident with the process, I facilitated the sessions with the process taking a few iterations to the final production of 'this is how I would like to be treated at work'.

Some warm-up questions with which I start the process (see the following list) give us a positive basis for opening up with safety and respect.

1. Which colleagues uplift you at work?
2. What is it specifically about them that uplifts you? (Specificity is key here, as we are narrowing and defining the traits.)
3. Think of a person or people who drain you (we don't share names for this question during our facilitated sessions for obvious reasons).
4. What is it specifically about them that drains you? (Specificity is key here, as we are narrowing and defining the traits.)

5. What types of work-related activities motivate you?

These questions are some examples of how I might start a session on 'Teach me how to treat you'. Spend some time answering them for yourself. What do your answers reveal?

Colleagues who uplift us

How do you feel about and around the colleagues who uplift you? What resilient behaviours and positive traits do they demonstrate? Do you feel confident and assured around them? Is there an element of safety? Do you feel you are able to be open and, at times, vulnerable with them. Do they inspire you and keep you grounded? Do they breed optimism and humour at just the right time? Do you feel listened to? Do they make you smile and is their energy infectious?

Now that was some list of questions. We love to define the characteristics of positive people using an array of leadership styles, but ultimately it is down to how we feel around others and the perceptions we form. We have heard the phrase: 'Leave people better than you found them', as in take: 'Take responsibility for how you contribute to how others feel'. Have agency in how you choose to show up. Elevate the positive states of being rather than waiting for others to elevate them for you. Be the change you want to see before you allow the three cancers (comparing, criticising and complaining) of the mind to dictate your experience and interactions with others.

Colleagues who drain us

How do you they leave you feeling? Do they complain, criticise and judge? Do they gossip? Are they stuck in a cycle? Is everything pessimistic? Do they offload before they engage in any listening? Do their voices dominate conversations? How do others respond to them? Do they self-reflect? Do they have a sense of entitlement? Are they part of the change they want to see? Are most interactions negative? Do you feel safe around them? Do you feel a sense of trust?

Stark questions compared with those about colleagues who uplift us. I feel a negative energy simply writing the questions. Most successful schools have more colleagues who uplift us than ones who drain us. However, it only takes one individual with lack of awareness to erode a culture. In Chapter 1, I mentioned a Harvard professor who has studied the negative contagion and its effects. It spreads like a contagion. It is caught whether you intend for it to be or not. We can't control how people think and behave but simply offer our requirements on how we wish to create a place full of care, culture and connection, and what the impact against the negative connotations associated with a poor culture are.

Sometimes the subtle negativity and I liken this to is the low-level disruption we refer to as hindering progress as much as high level can be as damaging as individuals who do not mask their dissatisfaction. There isn't the mechanism to call out such behaviors when they are not deemed as meeting the threshold. We can struggle to handle challenging conversations for a variety of reasons and let the subtle go, not realising the chipping away incessantly is just as damaging.

Here's a thought provoking question to think about: If the new Ofsted report cards wanted to evaluate culture, what would you want to introduce overnight? What would you need to start considering immediately?

The 'real' staff survey

Here are some more example questions that I ask to get a sense and feel of how staff *really* feel about culture. As with all of these example questions, you may wish to make a note of your answers.

1. Can you recall a time when you felt genuinely encouraged at work? What made it meaningful?
2. How often do you feel recognised for your efforts? What forms of recognition (public, private, tangible, verbal) resonate most with you?

3. What actions do you take to support a positive culture? Are there any obstacles preventing a stronger sense of teamwork?
4. What would improve communication and teamwork in your opinion?
5. What energises you the most? Are there specific activities or responsibilities that make you feel more engaged and motivated?
6. Do you have opportunities to feel joy and satisfaction? If not, what changes would help you feel more fulfilled in your role?
7. Have you thought about leaving the profession? What factors contribute to this feeling? What changes would make you want to stay?

In essence what we are establishing is how staff would like to receive and contribute to culture. We can interpret from the answers a collective 'Teach me how to treat you' before we establish individual ones. The 'real' staff survey starts at the professional curiosity level about how people truly feel or as close to. It removes the negative bias associated with annual staff surveys. It wants to connect with people from a genuine starting point and therefore removes the first barrier to engagement and trust. Localised staff surveys benefit from the rich data we wish to receive. Investing time and space to allow for a 'real' staff survey and a 'real' staff voice is one way to ensure staff feel valued.

In turn, the first step in the process opens the next part, which is the individual 'Teach me how to treat you'. At this point staff are engaged and understand the 'why' and 'how' of the process. The 'why' is simple: 'We value you, your work, your efforts, your dedication, your expertise, your feelings, your thoughts.' We want to find out how we as a collective can strengthen our care, connection and culture and so a 'real' staff survey carried out by an independent objective 'real' person is one way to capture this. Of course, you could shape this process and the questions. What questions would you love to be asked? Here we set out our why and the tone is collaborative and safe. We are offering, inviting staff into, the process and asking if they would like to contribute to a question they would like to be asked. We know how self-efficacy raises positive states of being. The answers are shared transparently, professional curiosity a must. The difference with the real staff survey is that it includes you. It is not an additional task to be completed and actioned by you alone. Your thoughts and feelings are captured within the 'real' staff survey for you. You are as much a colleague as anyone else and yet we are left with the responsibility to engage staff with a survey and action the recommendations as a separate role within the school.

What you are encouraging is an openness to see things how they *really* are. Staff appreciate this. I have carried out many 'real' staff surveys and not experienced disengagement or cynicism, but honest reflections and desire for strengthening what currently exists. How we frame honest feedback is that it remains anonymous unless someone wishes to share it personally from themselves.

Working through how people perceive culture and how they wish to be treated does require professional and emotional intelligence. We are human after all and must at times understand that feedback is not a slight on our efforts. This can be challenging when leaders believe that it is their sole responsibility to make sure everyone is satisfied. I am not going to delve into people pleasing, but unless you have removed the need for everyone to like you at the expense to yourself I would suggest doing some research and/or exploring this with a coach. It is very natural to want to be liked, but at what cost.

A strong 'treat me how to treat you' outlines professional courtesy. It makes the case that some decisions won't be liked – and that's okay. I won't always get it right – and that's okay. I will have to take my time on this – and that's okay. I won't be able to give you an answer immediately – and that's okay. I will have some radical candor with you from time to time – and that's okay.

What we should remember is that we are part of the process too. We don't have all the answers. We are only a lone island if we cut off the support networks we need from those around us believing that leadership is lonely and we must have it all together. We are not infallible. I have worked with staff teams on breaking the myths they have about the leaders in school and build the cohesiveness across colleagues as one. Without intentionally knowing it, we can contribute to the divide. Having staff aware of leaders 'Teach me how to treat you' is always

The Human Side of School Leadership

eye-opening. Often, we dispel a lot of limiting assumptions just with one activity alone.

Before I give you an example (WAGOLL) of my 'treat me how to teach you', the case study you'll find here is an example of the first school I supported in the launch of Balance:ed. A lovely warm school, full of dedication and commitment to improving outcomes and culture.

> **Case study: Whitechapel C of E primary school – a culture shift from compliance to connection**
>
> Whitechapel C of E primary school was already a place rooted in care. But like many schools, their systems – particularly performance management – weren't quite matching the culture they were trying to cultivate. Leadership carried the weight. Conversations felt evaluative rather than expansive. Everyone was doing their best, but the framework wasn't helping them to thrive.
>
> When I began working with the leadership team, we didn't start with policies. We started with people.
>
> The first piece of work was with the senior leadership team using a reflective framework I call 'Teach me how to treat you'. It's a deceptively simple idea with a transformative impact. Each leader took time to consider and share how they work best, how they like to be challenged, how they want to receive feedback, and how they know they are valued. These weren't surface answers. They were honest, grounded and deeply personal. For many, it was the first time they had ever been asked. And it changed everything.
>
> With the SLT (Senior Leadership Team) modelling vulnerability and clarity, we extended this same work to wider staff teams. We supported everyone – teachers, support staff, admin, site – to reflect and share in pairs and groups. What emerged was a rich understanding not just of how people work, but why. Colleagues who had worked side by side for years suddenly had new insight into one another. Compassion grew. Language shifted.
>
> From there, we turned to performance management. The school was brave in their decision to completely revamp the process. Rather

than target-setting from the top down, we rebuilt the model from the inside out. At the centre were the Most Important Questions (MIQs), designed to place voice, agency and ownership back into the hands of staff.

Everyone – from ECTs (Early Career Teachers) to SLTs – was invited to articulate three core experiences they wanted to focus on that year. These could be professional (e.g. improving teaching practice, developing middle leadership), personal (e.g. working towards a qualification, balancing work and parenting), or relational (e.g. improving collaboration, mentoring others). Each MIQ was tied to a strength, not a deficit. The question wasn't 'What do you need to fix?' but 'What do you want to grow into?'

Check-ins happened each half term, but not as appraisals. These were coaching-style conversations, facilitated by leaders who now knew the preferred communication styles, motivators and triggers of their team. Conversations deepened. Staff felt safe enough to say what wasn't working and confident enough to articulate what they needed. Performance didn't dip; it soared. But not because people were told to improve. Because they chose to.

What was remarkable was the shift in ownership. Leaders no longer had to drive everything. Staff came prepared, reflective and motivated. There was a shared understanding of mutual responsibility for culture. Everyone had skin in the game.

A teacher said, 'For the first time, this doesn't feel like something done to me. It feels like something I get to shape.'

A middle leader reflected, 'I know my team better now. I don't have to guess what matters to them – I've heard it.'

And one SLT member shared, 'The pressure has lifted. I'm not holding all of it anymore. We're holding it together.'

This is what a teacher-led, values-aligned, human-first model can look like in action. It's not soft. It's strategic. And it works.

Whitechapel didn't just change a system. They changed their story. From compliance to connection. From performance management to professional growth. From holding it all together to sharing the weight.

And that is what true leadership looks like – not in control, but in collaboration. Not managing people, but enabling them. And not afraid to start again when something no longer serves the people it was designed for.

Their courage and commitment to building a school culture where people feel known, hear and empowered continues to ripple out. And I am grateful to have walked that journey alongside them.

An example of a 'Teach me how to treat you' from different headteachers

- I find it helpful when I am given some time to decompress first thing in the morning so that I can set the tone for the day. Twenty minutes is all I need.
- I find it helpful that I have some time to decide. I like it when I have time to process and weigh everything up.
- I find it helpful if I am also asked how I am when I take the time to ask everyone.
- I find it helpful when people can see I am overwhelmed or over-worked, and I am given a little bit of space on the day to get my head down.
- I find it helpful that you respect the sign on the door which indicates that I need to work on something important.
- I find it helpful that my time of arrival is not highlighted as an issue when I have a small family to drop to nursery in the morning.
- I find it helpful when we have lots of humor and laughter but when the agenda starts, we all respect time.
- I find it helpful that if you need me to respond to something you email me or write it on a sticky note, because a passing comment on the corridor can be forgotten easily.

Teach me how to treat you

We are removing the frustraters, those small incidents that build up each day and can often leave us feeling depleted. Outlining what works for us professionally includes our individuality and feelings of belonging. It says *I matter too*. The outline does not have to be long; it just needs to include your top six frustraters normally. I encourage senior leaders to display their teams in their offices and reference them during one-to-ones, check-ins or performance reviews. I encourage the head teacher to share with SLTs and the chair of governors.

Reflection exercise

Write your own version of 'Teach me how to treat you' in a notebook. Remember to keep it as positive as you can. We tread a fine line between professional courtesy and demands that may look selfish but are in fact the opposite. We are asking for a little help in the day-to-day. Once you feel comfortable with your version, share it with your senior leadership team. Talk through the concept and feel of explicitly outlining your needs of professional regard. Engage in the same activity with your team and display these on the wall as I encourage senior leaders to do so that you are reminded of how important it is to elevate each other's experience. The impact: a stronger bond with your team, an outline that prevents misunderstandings, higher levels of happy hormone oxytocin, particularly when you are engaged in the activity of writing and sharing. Let me know how you found the process or reach out to book my service facilitating 'Teach me how to treat you' sessions. I often create away days for teams to build and strengthen cohesiveness and a better understanding of the mission, vision and values of the school. Get in touch if this is something you feel would benefit.

The Human Side of School Leadership

Chapter summary

This chapter is where connection stops being an abstract idea and becomes something you can actually pick up, use and embed into the way you lead. 'Teach me how to treat you' isn't a gimmick; it's a way of working that gives people permission to be clear about who they are, what matters to them and how they want to be treated. And it gives leaders the same permission in return.

Most leaders I work with can list their values without hesitation: kind, compassionate, driven, committed. But when I ask if those values are truly felt by the people they lead, the pause says it all. It's one thing to believe you're a certain kind of leader; it's another for others to actually experience you that way. That's the real work: bridging the gap between intention and impact.

In this chapter, I ask you to let go of the idea that your role has to be guarded, distant or wrapped in formality. Instead, we talk about how to bring down some of those walls, how to have honest conversations that don't just maintain the status quo but actively shape the culture you want.

We cover practical ways to do this: using warm-up questions to break through surface-level interactions; replacing traditional meeting openers with conversations about connection; running real culture audits; and asking questions that reveal more than a staff survey ever could. These are tools that don't just *do* wellbeing; they *create* it.

I share the work we did at Whitechapel Church of England primary school, where we started with leaders, moved through teams and reimagined performance management as a teacher-led professional development process driven by MIQs (Most Important Questions). Suddenly, everyone knew each other's preferred way of working, what motivated them, how they wanted to grow, and what they cared about both professionally and personally. It wasn't leadership dragging the process; it was everyone taking responsibility for their own experience and journey.

We also talk honestly about the reality of workplace dynamics – the colleagues who energise you, the ones who drain you, and the quiet undercurrents of negativity that can eat away at a team if they're left unspoken. By naming these, we take the sting out of them and free up space for the good stuff – trust, respect and curiosity.

Because at the heart of 'Teach me how to treat you' is this: people want to be understood. They want to feel seen not just for what they do, but for who they are. And when leaders create space for that, it changes everything. It's called belonging and belonging is a way of being and feeling.

Interlude 3
by Narinder Gill

> James Clear, author of *Atomic Habits* (2018), once said, 'You do not rise to the level of your goals. You fall to the level of your systems.' This perspective sits at the heart of what Narinder Gill (Educational Leader, author and coach) shares in the reflection that follows.

Narinder's reflection

This quote exists where reality meets hope, a space I've often found myself in throughout my career in education.

For years, I believed that high expectations could carry us through almost anything. In schools facing deep-seated challenges, it felt essential to believe in what was possible. But I realised that hope alone cannot support the weight of broken systems. Without proper conditions, even well-meaning expectations break down under pressure.

I've led schools where children arrived with stories of trauma and hardship. I've seen talented teachers falter under constant workload and accountability. I've also seen transformation happen not through quick fixes, but when we took the slower route of building systems that support people.

Wellbeing, I've learned, is not a programme we add on. It's how we show up within our systems. How we lead meetings, listen and foster safety in teams. How we respond when someone struggles not as an exception, but as part of everyday practice.

Interlude 3

At Elevate Trust, we embedded a coaching culture not because it sounded appealing, but because compassionate accountability had to be more than just words. We co-created curriculum not only to improve standards but to ensure every child saw themselves reflected in their learning. These were not surface solutions; they were systemic responses to complex communities.

For those of us who've navigated systems not designed with us in mind, Covey's quote hits close to home too. We know what it's like to carry high expectations while working within structures that resist change. We also recognise the power of reworking those systems for ourselves, for others and for the children observing.

When wellbeing is genuinely part of the culture, it isn't performative. It's embedded in how we make decisions, wield power and rebuild trust. It's the unseen structure that enables flourishing.

Expectations matter, but systems are what sustain us. If we're committed to wellbeing, we must go beyond resilience talk and focus on redesign not just for those who can keep going, but for everyone who deserves to belong.

This quote reminds me that when we create better systems, people don't have to burn out trying to survive broken ones. They can thrive.

4
Connecting questions and transforming meetings

> **Connecting question:** Who or what makes you forget about time?

What beautiful question to be asked. A way to find out more about you. A curious question, but a question that generates more curiosity with the answer. One that moves away from the traditional 'check-in' questions you may have experienced over the years, particularly if you have worked in a relational practice environment. The problem that often occurs is that 'check-in' questions, which I prefer to refer to as connecting questions, often become diluted over time into questions that don't stimulate deep thinking. The superficiality can take over and questions become more about what your favorite childhood dinner was or what you watched over the weekend.

Moving beyond superficial check-ins

If we desire our teams to know more about each other beyond the superficial, to develop a stronger bond and to work collaboratively and cohesively together, then we need to think about how our meetings are structured to allow time and investment in others. Think developing a strong sense of belonging that every people strategy has a pillar dedicated to now. One of the buzzwords linked to inclusion. A sense of belonging can be very individual. We know that we have an epidemic of loneliness the likes we have not experienced before, and I often ask as mentioned in Chapter 3: 'What is the prevalence of loneliness in your organisation?'

We need connection to thrive, and loneliness sets us into survival mode. We need to move beyond policy to tangible aspects of connection. A policy could simply set out all the ways we connect to thrive or how we embed opportunities to connect on a daily or weekly basis. Sound too operational? Well in a way it is, but this is what colleagues need to know: that a people strategy needs to be translated into everyday practices, taking the mission, vision and values and enacting it into the fabric of school life. Relationships matter more than we think.

Psychological safety through connection

Psychological safety is not in the absence of threat but in the presence of connection. Using our everyday interactions to build and strengthen the presence of connection and then intentionally using the opportunities for more formal interactions to further build a strong sense of belonging such as meetings where leaders spend most of their time within. Shaping the intentions of giving time to creating connection sets the tone for culture. Yes, you have business at hand but when people have time to think, share, strengthen, are valued, heard and understood, then their quality of thinking improves.

> **Reflection exercise 1**
>
> I want you to remember a time when you sat in a meeting that was terrible. What were the characteristics of that meeting? Spend a few moments recalling it. How did people interact? How did they contribute? How was it chaired? What was achieved?
>
> Now think about the feelings this terrible meeting generated. What did you feel? What about others in the meeting? Did you identify feelings of frustration, low patience, overwhelm, lack of motivation and engagement? Did you feel as though it was a waste of valuable time

Connecting questions and transforming meetings

or parts of it were a waste? How many times were individuals interrupted? How long did presenters spend talking and so on?

Now I want you to think of a positive meeting. What were the characteristics of that meeting? Spend a few moments recalling it. How did people interact? How did they contribute? How was it chaired? What was achieved? Now think about the feelings this meeting generated. What did you feel? What about others in the meeting? Did you identify feelings of regard, patience, understanding, motivation and engagement? Did you have opportunities to share and collaborate? Was it chaired equitably? Were laptops and phones away? Did it spark curiosity and did you manage to stay curious. Did you come away feeling better connected with everyone around you?

Transforming meetings into ones where connection thrives and quality thinking is unleased is one to instill and a quick and easy win. Using connecting questions is one way to promote an acute sense of belonging even if people feel a little bit disconnected from the overall picture and dissonance with direction, culture or outcomes to be achieved. I always advise people to do one thing well that does not sit in insolation with the rest of the meeting.

Reflection exercise 2

Take a few moments to close your eyes and imagine a meeting you would love to be in and, yes, I did say 'love'. Just feel yourself within one. Open your eyes, keep hold of the feelings and thoughts it generates and take some time to write down your answers to the following questions.

1. How do you want people to feel in meetings within your setting?
2. What do you want them to have accomplished?
3. What principles allow colleagues to feel the above?
4. How would you communicate these?

Now let's turn this into a reality.

Connecting questions of check-ins

In terms of practicality, we would run a meeting in a format that allows intentional connection to flourish. Start with a connecting question only once you have established this format prior with colleagues, so they understand the process. Choose a connecting question that will engage thinking, curiosity and care. To create care, culture and connection we frame the meetings in terms of rounds. Each person is invited to respond to the question one at a time with no interruptions (this point is one of the most important points). To be valued, seen and heard we need our thinking to matter uninterrupted. If you only introduce one thing it would be this. I have supported many teams in building cohesion and deepening bonds, and I often find, through no fault of their own, so much interruption within meetings or conversations because that's how we have learned to operate in a busy environment. Yet when we look at the notion of interrupting, it implies that my thinking matters more than yours. In fact, according to Nancy Kline *Time to Think* (1991), interruptions stop thinking altogether when, in fact, what we want is quality thought. I always refer to the sentence from *Time to Think* 'How far can you go in your thinking before you need mine?'

In terms of set up. I will provide an outline to facilitate connecting questions for ease and simplicity. Remember, I want to leave you with tangible and tactical ways to embed.

Welcome everyone to the meeting, ensuring you make eye contact with all those you greet individually. If you can't greet everyone individually due to the size of your meeting, be sure to make eye contact with everyone during the meeting. You are acknowledging them and their presence. This is powerful. It says 'Welcome' and 'We need you and your thinking at this table'. You introduce a connecting question and allow people time to process this, remembering that process time is different for diverse thinkers. It offers the opportunity to pause, reflect, gather thoughts and most important of all to *think* through the question.

Safety doesn't jump straight into the answers. The tone we are setting up from the outset is that thinking is valuable, and quality thinking is important to us. We know that quality of thought is linked to quality of performance and quality of being. You see, wellbeing is culture and culture is tone, and tone is the implied message, and the message is the vision, and the vision is the mission, and the mission comes alive through values. Needed a pause after that sentence. To create connection to support thinking and in turn value colleagues, we intentionally create a different type of meeting.

I want you to think about the last time *your* thinking flourished, where time and the agenda weren't constraints. We've become time fixated and agenda orientated in the busyness of time and getting the job done. We thrive and flourish on connection; we become alive and passionate when our minds are free to roam as thinkers, when we essentially have time to think.

Five transformative connecting questions

When you introduce the connecting question, you pause as mentioned to allow the question to settle in people's minds. You invite someone to start and follow the round from the next person. Depending on your agenda you will need to set aside quality time to become accustomed to connecting questions and the length of time-sharing individual thoughts. Some great connecting questions I have used in meetings are as follows.

1. How would you like to be encouraged right now?
2. What are you most proud of in your personal or professional life?
3. What brings you most joy?
4. Who or what makes you forget about time?
5. What is your life like when it is balanced?

You can see the variety of the type of questions. They move beyond the superficial questions around 'What is your favourite meal?' and so on. They offer a richness of understanding, offer gems of the other and spark a lot of curiosity and acceptance. The move is to go beyond the superficial and spark reflection in our colleagues. Moving to ignite thinking leads to introspection, which elevates positive states of being.

The Human Side of School Leadership

It is a way of being seen for who we are as opposed to just the title and role.

It is important to outline that the questions do require vulnerability. Psychological safety does need to be built for people to be open and honest. But we know that vulnerability is a magnet not a repellant. The question is how comfortable you are as a team to ask thought provoking and empowering questions.

Let's take each question in turn

1. *How would you like to be encouraged right now?*

What a beautiful question. It based on self-efficacy and introspection. It says I have autonomy to decide but interestingly it asks you to define what encouragement looks like for you. For the person asking the question it offers them an insight like no other question on what motivates them. Asking the question shows a genuine interest in the answer. In turn it is answered authentically when the time is taken to process it. Some might want their work to be acknowledged now and again, others may need some time to collaborate with other colleagues, for some it may be direct feedback.

How would *you* want to be encouraged right now? Take your time with this. Think about all the ways you would like to feel validated and appreciated for what and how you do what you do.

My answer (after I've heard yours, of course, with no interruptions) would be to be asked what I am working on now or what I intend to work on. My encouragement comes from someone being genuinely curious. I would like to hear encouragement through questions such as 'What can I do to help?' or 'What do you need from me?'

2. *What are you most proud of in your personal or professional life?*

This question invites the person to share elements of their deeper self. It doesn't really matter which element they choose to answer, it still provides an insight into what they perceive as their proudest. Curiosity

Connecting questions and transforming meetings

to ask the question and curiosity to hear the answer. No need to qualify the answer with a response but simply listening and absorbing. The listening itself is the response and acknowledgment.

What are *you* most proud of in your personal or professional life? Take the time to answer the question.

This question, for me, brings clarity to what truly matters. Professionally, it would be founding Balance:ed – a purposeful endeavour created in honour of my late husband. What began in grief transformed into a journey of impact, healing and meaningful service. It became not only a tribute to his memory but a living legacy that continues to shape others' lives.

On a personal level, my greatest pride lies in the legacy I hope to leave for my grandson, Isaac. He fills my heart with joy and purpose, and every choice I make is coloured by the desire to model compassion, resilience and love for him. Both show the impact of meaningful and profound relationships; connection sinks into the identity we hold personally and professionally.

3. What brings you most joy?

Turning the mind to the positive. Forcing the mind to think of the joy. What truly makes your heart sing? What fills you with happiness and a positive state of being? Is it in the simple pleasures of life or the big moments that take your breath away? Do you experience consistent moments of joy throughout your week, or do they come in beautiful, fleeting glimpses? Do you notice them when they happen, or do they pass by unnoticed in the busyness of your days? Again, the question invites a deeper reflection and deeper insight. It calls us to slow down just enough to notice the small sparks that light us up from the inside out. It's a question that not only reveals what we value but reminds us that joy is a state worth cultivating something we deserve, even in the most demanding seasons of life.

What brings *you* most joy? What does the answer reveal when you have to dig, when you really stop and sit with the question rather than rushing to respond? For some, it shows the lack of consistent things that bring us joy – a quiet call to stop and pause, to take stock of what's missing. For others, it may be many things, layered and meaningful, but overshadowed by a lack of time, space or permission to experience them fully. And for some, they can't find *the most* not because it doesn't exist, but because life has become too full, too loud or too disconnected from what once mattered most.

4. Who or what makes you forget about time?

I love this question. I often ask this question during my keynotes. It is a fantastic connecting question and reveals so much about the other. People love talking about hobbies, passions, family, pets, holidays and so on – the things that make people light up as they speak. Forgetting time, though, goes beyond the passing of time by doing something enjoyable. It is a state of flow, where the mind is fully absorbed and hooked into something so enjoyable, so engaging, that everything else fades away. The curiosity of the question is as appealing as the answer; it opens a window into what truly matters, what energises, what brings peace.

So, who or what makes *you* forget about time? What would you say brings you into a state of flow? Could you pin this down to a single thing, or are you lucky enough to have a few things that offer you release from a busy mind, from the ever-growing to-do list, from the noise of the day-to-day? Take a moment to reflect on what those moments feel like. What does your body feel like? What does your breath do? Those are clues to what keeps you grounded and alive.

For me, it is reading. I've always been an avid reader from a young age. Seeing escapism from turbulent times. It was my go-to when my husband passed. A quiet companion that never needed explanation. I find solace, understanding, challenge, learning, soothing and every comfort you can name in the words on a page. It's not just about the content, it's about the sanctuary. Books have held me when nothing else could. They've offered mirrors when I needed to see myself, and windows when I needed to look beyond my world. The texture of a page, the rhythm of language, the stillness it invites – reading brings me back to myself, no matter how far I've strayed.

5. What is my life like when it is balanced?

If there ever was a question to make us stop and take stock, then this is the one. A question that holds a mirror up and asks us to really look.

What does balance even mean for *you*? Is it a sense of calm in your body, space in your diary, moments of joy without guilt? Is it feeling present in your own life rather than racing through it? For some, balance is a rhythm, not a destination – something fluid, shifting with seasons. For others, it's boundaries held, time protected, energy restored. When life is balanced, we notice things more. We breathe slower. We listen better. We laugh easier. It's not about *doing less*; it's about *being more*. More aligned, more grounded, more like us.

Work/life balance is something we all aim for. The balance between home and work is considered the epitome of a successful life. 'We must be effective at both' is a pressure we strive for and place upon ourselves. But have we ever stopped to ask ourselves what balance means and, most importantly, what balance means for us. The question invites us to set out the balance, to look inward on what truly matters to us. The question asked within a team gives you further insight into what areas mean balance along with the ideal balance for colleagues.

And for those in leadership, this question becomes even more important. A balanced leader leads differently. They model calm. They create space for others. They bring clarity in chaos. When leadership is balanced, teams feel it. They feel safer, more supported, more human. Because leadership isn't about doing it all; it's about showing what it looks like to lead from a place of wholeness.

For me, balance simply means less stress, a state where I can be fully present in both my work and home life without feeling torn between the two. It's about giving each the attention, time and commitment they deserve, without one overshadowing the other. Achieving balance requires intentionality; it means identifying the pinch points, the areas that trigger stress or overwhelm, and actively finding ways to reduce or even eliminate them. It's about consciously creating space and reclaiming time by rethinking priorities and refining how I navigate both work and home. Balance is not just a state of mind; it's a deliberate practice of alignment, where my energy flows where it's needed most, enabling me to thrive in both spaces without compromise.

And so, I invite you to answer this question. What is my life like when it is balanced? What would you hope your colleagues would say? What would you do if your team feels there is no balance, and this is detriment to their wellbeing?

These examples of connecting questions are only a sample to use within your meetings. These questions are designed to open up dialogue, encourage reflection and build deeper understanding among team members. They serve as gentle prompts to explore thoughts, feelings and experiences that might otherwise remain unspoken. However, for these questions to be truly effective, psychological safety must be present for colleagues to answer each question authentically and honestly. Without a foundation of trust and safety, team members may hold back, offering surface-level responses instead of genuine insights.

Cultivating trust and openness

Psychological safety is the cornerstone of meaningful dialogue. It is what allows individuals to feel secure enough to share openly without fear of judgement, repercussion or dismissal. It creates a space where vulnerability is not only accepted but encouraged. When colleagues know they are supported and respected, they are far more likely to engage in honest conversations that can lead to growth, understanding and stronger connections. This kind of environment does not happen by accident; it must be intentionally cultivated. Leaders and facilitators play a critical role in setting the tone, modeling openness and demonstrating that all voices are valued.

Building psychological safety starts with simple but powerful actions: actively listening when others speak; showing empathy towards

Connecting questions and transforming meetings

different perspectives; and responding with kindness and curiosity rather than criticism. It means addressing conflicts constructively and ensuring that everyone has an equal opportunity to contribute. This also involves recognising that mistakes and misunderstandings are part of the learning process and should be approached with patience and a willingness to learn, rather than blame.

In your meetings, as you use these connecting questions, it's important to be mindful of the atmosphere you create. Begin by setting clear expectations around respect and confidentiality. Reassure colleagues that their contributions are welcome and that the space is judgement-free. It might even be helpful to explicitly state that all responses are valued, regardless of differences in opinion or perspective. When individuals feel heard and respected, their willingness to share openly increases and the quality of dialogue deepens.

Additionally, consider starting with lighter, low-risk questions to build comfort before moving into more personal or reflective territory. This gradual approach allows team members to acclimatise to the process of sharing while still feeling secure. Over time, as trust builds, you may find that colleagues become more willing to engage with vulnerability, offering insights and reflections that contribute to collective learning and growth.

Ultimately, the goal of using connecting questions is not just to elicit responses but to foster a culture of trust and openness. When psychological safety is prioritised, meetings transform from mere exchanges of information to genuine opportunities for connection and understanding. This shift not only strengthens team dynamics but also enhances overall wellbeing, as individuals feel seen, heard and valued for who they are and what they bring to the table.

The examples of connecting questions are just a starting point, but with the right environment they have the potential to unlock powerful conversations that drive growth, unity and a deeper sense of belonging within your team.

> **Reflection exercise**
>
> Take a moment to think about a recent meeting or conversation where you asked a connecting question. Reflect honestly on the environment. Was there enough psychological safety for real answers to emerge?
>
> **Describe the atmosphere:**
>
> - Was there openness?
> - Did everyone seem comfortable sharing their thoughts?
> - Were people speaking freely, or did it feel guarded?
>
> **Consider your role:**
>
> - How did you show up in that space?
> - Were you fully present, actively listening and showing empathy?
> - Did you set the tone for openness and non-judgement?
>
> **Identify one shift:**
>
> - What is one small shift you could make to enhance psychological safety next time?
> - Could it be a clearer introduction to set expectations? More acknowledgement of contributions? Greater patience in listening?
>
> Write down your reflections and your chosen shift. Keep it visible before your next meeting as a reminder of the impact you want to create.

Creating space for real connection isn't always easy, but it's always worth it. When people feel safe enough to be themselves, the conversations that follow are richer, the trust is deeper and the sense of belonging is undeniable. And that, ultimately, is what transforms teams not just the questions we ask, but the space we create for the answers.

Connecting questions and transforming meetings

Chapter summary

Throughout this chapter, we've explored how connecting questions can serve as powerful tools for deepening understanding and building genuine relationships within our teams. These questions are not just prompts for discussion; they are opportunities to break through the surface and really see each other. But for that to happen authentically, psychological safety needs to be present. Without it, people hold back, offering only what feels safe rather than what is real.

Psychological safety isn't a nice-to-have; it's essential. It's the invisible thread that allows colleagues to speak freely, to share their thoughts and feelings without fear of judgement or repercussion. When we create an environment where people feel safe, we give them permission to show up fully to admit struggles, to share ideas and to be honest about what's really going on. In the absence of that safety, conversations stay at the surface and true connection is lost.

Building that kind of space takes intention. It means actively listening – not just hearing words but really absorbing what's being said. It means responding with empathy, especially when perspectives differ or when someone shares something difficult. It's about setting the tone that mistakes are part of learning, not moments for blame. And, most importantly, it's about modeling the kind of openness and vulnerability you hope to see in others. When you show up authentically, you invite others to do the same.

As you reflect on this chapter, think about your own environments, your team meetings, your one-on-one conversations, even casual chats in the hallway. Where is there space for people to be real? Where might fear of judgement be holding people back? The connecting questions are only as powerful as the space you create for them. If psychological safety is present, those questions can transform conversations, turning them into moments of genuine understanding and trust.

Interlude 4
by Sufian Sadiq

> Malcolm X, a Black African-American civil rights leader, once said, 'Education is the passport to the future, for tomorrow belongs to those who prepare for it today … Real power comes from ordinary people who refuse to remain silent.' This perspective sits at the heart of what Sufian Sadiq (Chief Talent and Transformation Officer and speaker) shares in the reflection that follows.

Sufian's reflection

There are quotes that inspire you, and then there are quotes that live inside you. For me, Malcolm X's words fall into the latter category. They are not something I pull out for speeches or sprinkle into training slides. They are something I return to, in the quiet moments, often when the noise of leadership and politics is deafening, when my energy is gone, when I question if I can keep going.

'Education is the passport to the future.' That line has carried me from my childhood to where I am today. I grew up in a place where money may have been scarce, but aspiration was not. Our parents did not let us give in to our circumstances. They said: strive, push, learn, keep going. And yet, the system was not built to see me. I did not see myself reflected in the books we read or the people who taught us.

That is why Malcolm's words resonate so deeply. Education, for me, has always been about dignity as much as it is about knowledge. It is a passport, yes, but passports only matter if the borders open. For too many young people, the system stamps 'Not for you' long before their journey even begins. That contradiction, the promise of education versus the reality of inequality, is what I refuse to stay silent about.

Interlude 4

And this is where the second part of Malcolm's quote lands so powerfully for me: 'Real power comes from ordinary people who refuse to remain silent.' That is not a line for the history books. That is a line for the staffroom on a grey Monday morning. It is for the leader who is tired of being asked to do more with less. It is for the teacher who wonders if they can possibly face another year. It is for the CEO trying to hold the vision when the questions never stop.

Let me say this as plainly as I can: you do not need to be a hero to change lives. You do not need to carry it all. The power is not in some grand act. It is in the daily choices, to notice a student who is struggling, to offer kindness instead of judgement, to challenge injustice even when it is unpopular. It is as simple as liking a post on social media by a colleague who is calling out inequality. These are the things that build culture. These are the things that sustain hope.

I know the pressure you feel. I live it too. The late nights, the constant demands, the sense that no matter how much you give, it will never be enough. I have said it before: I often live on limited sleep, and that is the cost of choosing a life of service. But I have also learned, the hard way, that service without wellbeing is not sustainable. You cannot pour from an empty cup.

We need to stop treating wellbeing as a luxury, a nice to have. It is the foundation. If you are broken, burnt out, disconnected from your purpose, then your leadership will not be life-giving to anyone else. Sometimes the most radical and courageous act you can do as a leader is to rest. To stop. To breathe. To model that you, too, are human.

Angie Browne, whose work on equity has deeply influenced me, once said something on her *Nothing without us* podcast that has stayed with me: 'Wellbeing is not about what you add on, it is about how you lead.' That truth has shifted the way I see my own role. Leadership is not about pretending we are invincible. It is about leading with honesty, with vulnerability, with the courage to say: I am tired, but I still believe.

Because culture is not built in policies or frameworks. It is built in those raw, human moments. When a teacher feels safe enough to admit they are struggling without fear of judgement. When a leader chooses to prioritise compassion over compliance. When we make space for people to bring their whole selves, not the polished version, but the real one. That is when culture shifts.

So if you are reading this and you feel at the end of your rope, I want you to hear this: your exhaustion is not a failure. It is evidence that you care, that you have been giving, that you have been holding the line. Do not despise that tiredness. Honour it. And then take the time you need to renew.

The future belongs to those who prepare today. And preparing today does not always mean pushing harder. Sometimes it means pulling back, re-rooting yourself in purpose, finding again the joy that brought you into education in the first

The Human Side of School Leadership

place. Preparing today means protecting your own wellbeing so you can continue to serve with integrity tomorrow.

Malcolm X did not live to see the full fruit of his vision. But he planted seeds, and those seeds are still growing. That is what we do too. We may not see the long-term outcomes of our labour. But every act of care, every courageous truth, every moment we choose integrity over silence, those are seeds. And they matter.

Education is our passport to the future. Let us not give up on today. Not because it is easy, but because tomorrow belongs to the young people watching us. They are learning not just from what we teach, but from how we live. And the greatest lesson we can give them is this: ordinary people, honest people, tired people, can still hold extraordinary power when they refuse to remain silent.

So if you are the teacher wondering if you can get through another year, if you are the leader holding together a vision when everyone is looking to you for answers, if you are the colleague who feels invisible in the noise of the system, hear me clearly: *you are not alone.*

Take rest without guilt. Lean into your community. Speak your truth even if your voice shakes. Your presence, your integrity, your refusal to stay silent, these things matter more than you can imagine.

The system may not always see you, but I see you. Others see you. And more importantly, the children and young people you serve, they see you. They carry your words, your gestures, your belief in them, into their futures.

So do not give up. Breathe. Stand tall, even if your knees are shaking. Tomorrow belongs to those who prepare today, and by simply showing up with courage and honesty.

5
Performance management: A shift worth making

> **Connecting question:** What does performance mean to you?

Performance management is the process of holding you accountable to unrealistic expectations and targets – a conversation that takes place once a year to set targets to motivate you towards success as deemed by senior leaders or governors. Now let's move away from the cynical definition to Michael Armstrong's book *Armstrong's Handbook of Performance Management* (2017).

Armstrong (2017) defines performance management as 'a systematic process for improving organisational performance by developing the performance of individuals and teams. It is a means of getting better results by understanding and managing performance within an agreed framework of planned goals, standards and competency requirements'.

The reality behind the theory

In essence, it's a system for driving improvement in teaching and learning alongside outcomes – a framework that is supposed to hold educators to account while also supporting their professional growth. An accountable system. One that is often presented as methodical and objective but can be quite subjective depending on the needs of the school, the interpretation of its leaders, and those carrying out the review and evaluation of performance against a set of metrics. These metrics are intended to improve overall outcomes, but how often do they reflect the complexities of classroom teaching, student engagement and the day-to-day realities educators face?

What comes to mind when you think about performance management? An outdated system, perhaps. Management for the sake of management. A paper trail to prove compliance. Target setting, data scrutiny, evidence gathering – often towards unrealistic or disconnected targets. It can feel mechanical, clinical even, rather than supportive or developmental. For many, it's synonymous with bureaucracy and box-ticking exercises that seem far removed from the passion and purpose of teaching.

Questioning the status quo

What was your first experience of performance management? I ask this because I am yet to recall an example of truly productive performance management during my career. Schools and academies often adopt their local authority's performance management policy with little question or adaptation to their unique culture or needs. The governors typically pass the policy through without much scrutiny, accepting it as the norm part of the 'it has always been done like this' mentality. It's just another document in a pile of documents that rarely get revisited or challenged. We carry on, year after year, cycling through objectives and reviews, often with little reflection on the process itself or its actual impact on teaching and learning.

Again, we are yet to truly scrutinise the policy of scrutiny itself. Although many schools have moved away from the traditional performance management model to a more progressive professional development model, there are still many that cling to the old ways. It's almost as if shifting away from it would signify a loss of control or an abandonment of accountability. But I wonder: Are we measuring what really matters? Or are we simply following the well-worn path of compliance because it's what we know?

When was the last time you had the opportunity the real opportunity to evaluate the purpose and effectiveness of your performance management or professional development policy? Not just a tickbox review or a

Performance management: A shift worth making

brief mention in a leadership meeting, but an honest, reflective conversation about its purpose, its alignment with your school's mission, and its impact on staff morale and student outcomes. Just as time is taken to ensure that your vision and values align with the mission, so it needs to be with any policy whose purpose it is to advance performance and outcomes. Performance management is not just another process; it is single-handedly one of the most important systems in your school. It directly impacts teaching quality, staff wellbeing, and, ultimately, student success. Yet, how often do we pause to ask if it's working? If it's inspiring growth, or simply policing practice?

Interestingly, research suggests that there is little to no correlation between performance management and motivation (Kuvaas, 2011; deNisi & Murphy, 2017). Think about that for a moment. A system designed to improve performance does not, in fact, improve motivation. Traditionally, the academic year starts with an initial meeting to define the school's objectives – objectives that are often lifted straight from the school or academy development plan. One objective might relate to pupil performance, driven by data and metrics that are largely out of the teacher's control. Finally, there is the 'personal objective', usually chosen by the reviewee, though often within tight parameters that leave little room for real professional curiosity or meaningful growth.

We go through the motions, set targets, gather evidence and review performance – often without questioning the process or its impact. But maybe it's time we did. Maybe it's time we reimagined performance management not as a tool for scrutiny, but as a pathway for growth. Not as a method of compliance, but as a true driver of development. Imagine the difference that could make not just for staff, but for students too.

When we think about performance management in schools, it's often framed as an essential mechanism for accountability and improvement. On paper, it's intended to identify strengths, address areas for development, and ultimately improve teaching and learning outcomes. But the reality, as many of us have experienced, is far less inspiring. In fact, research increasingly suggests that the traditional approach to performance management is not only ineffective but may also be counterproductive.

The role of intrinsic motivation

One of the key issues with conventional performance management systems is their limited impact on teacher motivation. As Armstrong (2017) notes, while performance management is often positioned as a developmental process, in practice it can easily become mechanistic – focused on compliance rather than connection. Kuvaas (2011) supports this view, finding that traditional appraisal systems frequently fail to engage employees meaningfully, offering little to no improvement in motivation or performance. When the focus shifts towards accountability targets and evidence gathering, the sense of professional autonomy and purpose diminishes. This resonates deeply with what so many leaders and teachers express – the feeling that performance management discussions are more about fulfilling procedural requirements than fostering genuine growth or reflection.

It doesn't stop there. The assumption that performance management directly drives educational improvement has long been challenged. DeNisi and Murphy (2017) argue that despite decades of refinement, these systems still struggle to deliver meaningful or sustained improvements in performance. Their research highlights how overly structured or evaluative systems can stifle innovation and reduce intrinsic motivation, especially in professions driven by purpose, like education. These findings raise an important question: If performance management, in its traditional form, fails to enhance either teacher motivation or learning outcomes, is it time we redefined what progress and accountability should truly look like in our schools?

Another glaring flaw in traditional performance management is the subjectivity and potential bias that can creep into evaluations. Many systems rely heavily on value-added models to assess teacher effectiveness, despite long-standing concerns about their fairness and accuracy. Value-added models attempt to measure a teacher's impact on student learning based on test scores and other metrics, but it is often criticised for failing to account for variables outside of the teacher's control – e.g. socio-economic factors or varying student needs. Critics argue that this method not only misrepresents teacher performance but also unfairly penalises those working in more challenging environments (see Amrein-Beardsley, 2014). It's something I have seen firsthand – the feeling of being judged on criteria that don't always reflect the reality of the classroom.

From compliance to growth

There's also the issue of wellbeing. We talk about supporting teacher mental health and reducing burnout, yet the high-stakes nature of performance management often does the opposite. The constant pressure to meet targets, the data scrutiny and the evidence-gathering can create environments where teachers feel more scrutinised than supported. Although there is limited large-scale research directly linking PM to teacher burnout, anecdotal evidence and smaller studies indicate that the stress associated with high-stakes evaluations can significantly impact teacher wellbeing. It's a contradiction I've always struggled with. How can we expect teachers to thrive when the very systems designed to support improvement often feel punitive?

And then there's the bigger question: Does any of this benefit students? Surprisingly, despite all the emphasis on performance management as a lever for student success, there is limited evidence to suggest that traditional performance management approaches lead to improved student outcomes. We pour time and resources into these structures, believing they drive progress, yet the data doesn't seem to back this up. It makes me wonder if we're focusing our energy in the wrong places polishing systems that, at their core, may not be delivering the impact we intend.

All of this raises serious questions about the way we think about performance management in schools. If it's not motivating teachers, if it's not improving outcomes, and if it's contributing to stress rather than alleviating it, then maybe it's time for a change. Perhaps we need to rethink not just *how* we do performance management, but *why* we do it in the first place.

Clear motivation to improve professionally must come from within, nurtured by a deep sense of purpose and a genuine desire to grow and evolve. However, that internal drive flourishes best within an environment that actively encourages learning and accepts failure as part of the developmental process. When educators feel safe to take risks, reflect on their practice and learn from their mistakes without the looming fear of punitive measures, true growth is possible. We know all too well the consequences and impact of high-stakes accountability how it narrows focus, heightens anxiety and sometimes even stifles innovation. An environment that prioritises high support over high pressure flips this narrative, allowing reflective development and introspection to take root. In such spaces, mistakes become stepping stones, not stumbling blocks, and the journey towards improvement is seen as ongoing and evolving rather than rigid and prescriptive.

In education, we are fortunate to have many different models of leadership and diagnostics available to us – frameworks that help us assess ourselves against best practices and identify areas for growth. These models serve as mirrors, reflecting back both our strengths and our areas for development, guiding us to better understand our impact and effectiveness. But these tools are only as powerful as the mindset with which we approach them. If we engage with these diagnostics defensively or simply as compliance measures, we miss the opportunity for meaningful growth. Instead, when approached with openness and a willingness to learn, these models can be transformative, helping us to navigate the complexities of teaching and leadership with greater self-awareness and confidence.

Professional development

I am an advocate of professional challenge and growth – not the kind that comes from imposed targets or rigid evaluations, but the kind that emerges from deep, reflective practice. True growth, the kind that is sustainable and impactful, stems from an honest understanding of oneself. Deep reflection means knowing and owning what motivates you and drives your behaviour. It's about peeling back the layers and asking the hard questions: What are my strengths, and where do I need to grow? How do I respond under pressure, and what habits have I formed that either help or hinder my effectiveness? These reflections are not always comfortable, but they are necessary if we are to evolve and lead with authenticity and purpose.

What type of teacher or leader are you? How do your core beliefs, values and actions align with your philosophy of education? And, perhaps most importantly, how does your philosophy align with the environment in which you work? These questions are not just reflective exercises; they are foundational to your practice. When your philosophy and your environment are in harmony, your work feels purposeful and energising. When they are not, it can feel like pushing against the tide exhausting, unsustainable and misaligned. Understanding this alignment (or lack thereof) is crucial, as it shapes not only your experience but also your effectiveness and impact.

Creating space for this kind of introspection requires intention. It means carving out time to step back, reflect and consider not just *what* you are doing, but *why* you are doing it. It's about identifying where you are thriving and where you are merely surviving, and then having the courage to address those disparities. Growth is not linear, nor is it always comfortable, but it is always worthwhile. When we create environments that support this kind of reflective practice, we don't just grow individually, we elevate the collective practice of our teams, our schools and ultimately the learning experiences of our students.

Balancing autonomy and accountability

Autonomy and accountability, and whether both can coexist – particularly in the context of performance management – is a delicate balancing act. It's about finding the right level of structure and flexibility within the system of performance evaluation. Too much rigidity, and it risks becoming a 'done to' process, something imposed rather than co-created. We know that a 'done to' approach can often demotivate and devalue colleagues, stripping away their sense of agency and ownership over their own professional journey. It reduces performance management to a checklist exercise, one that feels more like compliance than growth. On the other hand, a 'done with' approach, where evaluation is collaborative and reflective, tends to have the opposite effect. It invites dialogue, values input and respects the professional expertise of those involved. It is a shared journey towards improvement, one where the individual is an active participant rather than a passive recipient.

A system that values individuals for their experience and knowledge, while also recognising what motivates them both personally and professionally, creates space for genuine development. It allows colleagues to feel seen and understood – not just as employees filling a role, but as unique contributors with their own aspirations and strengths. This kind of system doesn't just measure performance; it nurtures it. It opens up opportunities for growth by acknowledging where someone is now, understanding where they want to go and collaboratively mapping out how to get there. In this environment, performance management transforms from a process of scrutiny to a platform for growth, driven by both accountability and meaningful autonomy.

As leaders, it is crucial to remember that we are not the gatekeepers of talent and growth; we are the gate openers. Our role is not to decide who is ready or worthy of development, but to create the pathways that allow growth to happen sometimes even before someone is entirely ready. It's about believing in potential and providing the opportunities for it to be realised, even if the person themselves is still building their confidence. Leadership is about nurturing talent, not rationing it. It is a privilege to support growth and enable development, whether we deem the person ready or not. In fact, sometimes the greatest transformations happen when someone is given the chance to step up before they feel fully prepared. That leap of faith both from the leader and the individual can be the catalyst for profound learning and development.

The power of MIQs in performance management

One of life's fundamentals for me is the concept of the Most Important Questions (MIQs). It's a powerful tool I use not only in coaching but also in my school support work with performance management. These questions are designed to cut through the noise and get to the heart of what truly matters. They provoke reflection, challenge assumptions and inspire clarity. Asking the right questions at the right time can shift perspectives, unlock potential and drive meaningful action. In the realm of performance management, MIQs help colleagues connect with their deeper motivations and aspirations, encouraging them to think not just about what they are doing, but why they are doing it and what they want to achieve next.

When we lead with this mindset – valuing autonomy alongside accountability, opening gates instead of guarding them and asking the most important questions to inspire growth – we create cultures where performance management is not a task to be endured, but a journey to be embraced.

The three most important questions

Vishen Lakhiani (2016), in *The Code of the Extraordinary Mind*, introduces the concept of the three Most Important Questions to shift focus from traditional goal-setting, which often emphasises 'means goals' (like job titles or financial milestones), to 'end goals' that truly resonate with one's inner desires. He identifies three core areas to explore: experiences, growth and contribution.

Area 1: What experiences do you want to have?

This question encourages you to envision the life experiences that would bring you joy and fulfilment. It's about identifying what your soul craves, beyond material possessions or societal expectations.

The Human Side of School Leadership

Area 2: How do you want to grow?

Personal growth is essential for achieving the experiences you desire. This question prompts you to consider the skills, knowledge and personal development needed to evolve into the person capable of living your envisioned life.

Area 3: How do you want to contribute?

Contribution adds meaning to our lives. This question asks you to reflect on how you can give back to the world, utilising your experiences and growth to make a positive impact.

Lakhiani emphasises that by focusing on these three questions, individuals can create a life that's not only successful by external standards but also deeply satisfying and aligned with their true selves.

MIQs require us to take stock of the efficacy of both our personal and professional lives. They serve as a reflective tool that brings clarity to what truly matters, cutting through the noise of daily demands to reveal what we genuinely want to experience, how we want to grow and the impact we wish to have. At Mindvalley, Vishen Lakhiani's company dedicated to growth and development, every employee completes their own set of MIQs. This practice is not a mere formality; it is a foundational element of their culture. Employees are encouraged to articulate their biggest dreams and aspirations, and they are supported by their colleagues and leadership to actively pursue those experiences. This collective commitment to personal growth transforms the workplace into a hub of shared purpose and mutual support, where success is measured not just by performance metrics but by the fulfilment of individual and collective goals.

Inspired by this approach, I introduced MIQs to an early adopter of this concept, Whitechapel C of E primary school. What set this school apart was their bravery and willingness to step away from the traditional aspects of performance management. Rather than adhering to the usual rigid targets and box-ticking exercises, Whitechapel primary school chose to reimagine their performance management structure

Performance management: A shift worth making

entirely. They saw the potential of MIQs not just as an add-on, but as the backbone of their process a tool to drive meaningful reflection and purposeful growth, rather than mere compliance.

> **Case study 1: Whitechapel C of E primary school – redefining performance management with MIQs**
>
> When I first approached Whitechapel primary school with the idea of integrating MIQs into their performance management structure, it was met with a mixture of curiosity and cautious optimism. The leadership team, driven by a desire to create a more meaningful and empowering approach, took the bold step to move away from traditional performance management practices. Gone were the rigid, predetermined targets that often felt disconnected from the reality of teaching and learning. In their place, MIQs became the foundation for goal-setting and professional reflection.
>
> We began with an introductory session, where staff were invited to explore the Three Most Important Questions:
>
> 1. What experiences do you want to have?
> 2. How do you want to grow?
> 3. How do you want to contribute?
>
> To set the stage, I shared my example illustrating how clarity around these three questions helped employees not only articulate their aspirations but also to take tangible steps towards them with the support of their colleagues. It wasn't just about setting objectives; it was about meaningful introspection. Staff were encouraged to think deeply about what genuinely mattered to them, both inside and outside of the classroom.
>
> One teacher, for instance, spoke about her aspiration to develop expertise in trauma-informed practice. Her vision extended beyond mere skill acquisition; she wanted to transform how vulnerable students were supported in her school. Her growth objective was to

gain formal training in trauma-informed strategies, and her contribution goal was to lead staff workshops, sharing her knowledge to enhance collective practice. Framing her goals through MIQs made the path clear not just for her, but for her colleagues and leaders who committed to supporting her journey.

Leadership at Whitechapel embraced this model with genuine commitment. Performance management meetings evolved from checklist reviews to deep, reflective conversations. Staff were encouraged to revisit their answers regularly, reflecting on their progress and recalibrating their goals as needed. Leadership played an active role in supporting these journeys, facilitating connections, providing resources and celebrating milestones along the way. This wasn't just a shift in process; it was a shift in culture.

The impact was profound. Staff began to express greater clarity about their roles and their personal growth paths. Performance management no longer felt like an obligation; it felt like an opportunity for genuine development. Conversations during appraisal meetings shifted from data-driven scrutiny to discussions about purpose, growth and meaningful contribution. Staff left those meetings feeling heard, valued and motivated not just to meet targets, but to grow and contribute in ways that were deeply personal and professionally impactful.

Whitechapel's willingness to step away from the conventional approach to performance management was a bold move. By prioritising MIQs, they created a structure that not only measured performance but also fostered growth and fulfilment. Their journey serves as a testament to what is possible when performance management is reimagined not as a mechanism for compliance, but as a platform for purposeful development.

The leadership team at Whitechapel did not have to drive performance management as they had before. The entire dynamic shifted, transforming it from a top-down, SLT-led process to one that was

Performance management: A shift worth making

genuinely staff-led. This shift marked a fundamental change in how performance was understood and approached not as something managed by leadership alone, but as a collaborative process fuelled by the ambitions and reflections of the staff themselves. The introduction of MIQs as a central pillar of performance management brought a new sense of ownership and accountability to the process. Staff were no longer passive participants; they became active architects of their own professional growth.

To support this transformation, we introduced half-termly check-ins to hold open, meaningful conversations about their MIQs. These check-ins were designed not as formal evaluations, but as reflective dialogues spaces where staff could discuss their three key experiences, how they wished to grow in relation to these and the specific contributions they wanted to make. This structure allowed for honest reflection and forward planning, aligning personal aspirations with professional goals. One of the three MIQs was solely focused on the teaching and learning of their own practice, encouraging staff to think deeply about their impact in the classroom and the areas they wanted to develop further. These discussions were rich with insight, driving not just individual growth but collective improvement across the school.

Performance management at Whitechapel has since evolved into a system fully embedded for systemic growth and improvement. It is no longer seen as a compliance-driven process but as a meaningful journey of reflection and action. It is built on principles of voice and influence, where staff feel empowered to shape their own experiences at work. Most importantly, it is underpinned by genuine motivation a desire to grow, contribute and be part of something that values their strengths and supports their development. The process is now living and breathing, a true reflection of what happens when ownership is placed in the hands of those it matters to most.

The Human Side of School Leadership

> **Case study 2: Working with a CEO to transform executive team reflection**
>
> More recently, I had the opportunity to work alongside the CEO of a Multi-Academy Trust (MAT) who was eager to rethink how reflection and development were approached within his executive team. His vision was clear: to move away from surface-level discussions focused solely on data and operations, towards deeper, more meaningful, conversations about growth, leadership and collective purpose. Inspired by the work at Whitechapel C of E primary school, we began exploring how MIQs could be embedded into his approach with his executive team not just as a one-off exercise, but as part of a structured and ongoing process.
>
> Our first step was to sit down and map out what meaningful growth looked like for him and his senior leaders. The CEO and I spent time reflecting on his own MIQs, discussing what experiences he wanted to cultivate within his role, how he wished to grow as a leader and how he wanted to contribute not just to the strategic objectives of the Trust, but to the personal and professional growth of his executive team. This was not just an exercise; it was a deep dive into his purpose and vision – something that is so often missed in high-level leadership roles.
>
> After working through his own MIQs, the CEO expressed a strong desire to have deeper, more impactful conversations with his executive team. He felt that much of their dialogue had become transactional, focused on data, deadlines and compliance measures. He wanted to change that. Inspired by his own experience with MIQs, we designed a series of reflective sessions exclusively for his executive team, structured around the same three questions:
>
> 1. What experiences do you want to have as a leader within this executive team?
> 2. How do you want to grow in your role to better support our collective leadership?

Performance management: A shift worth making

3. How do you want to contribute to the culture and strategic direction we are building together?

These sessions were transformative. For many on the executive team, it was the first time they had been asked to reflect on their roles in such a personal and purposeful way. The conversations shifted from purely strategic check-ins to deeply reflective dialogues, allowing each leader to articulate not just their objectives, but their motivations, their challenges and their hopes for the future. One executive member remarked that it was 'the first time I've felt seen not just as a leader, but as a person'.

The CEO committed to holding these reflective sessions every half-term, making them a priority within their leadership calendar. He participated in each one not as a figure of authority, but as a participant, contributing his own reflections alongside his team. His presence wasn't about oversight; it was about understanding, connecting and growing together. This shift in dynamic was palpable. Trust grew, conversations deepened, and decision-making became more thoughtful and values-driven.

The impact was significant. The executive team reported feeling more connected to their roles and to each other. Conversations moved beyond surface-level reporting and into meaningful discussions about growth, shared goals and collective leadership. Performance was no longer viewed simply through metrics and outcomes but was reimagined as a journey of personal and professional growth, supported by honest reflection and shared accountability.

The experience with the CEO underscored something important: when executive leaders model reflective practice and genuinely engage with growth, it sets a tone for the entire team. It becomes part of the fabric of leadership – not just an add-on, but a fundamental way of working that fosters trust, development and collective purpose.

The Human Side of School Leadership

> **Reflection exercise**
>
> Think about the following questions. You could write down your answers or thoughts in a notebook, if you choose.
>
> - What purpose does your current performance management system really serve? Be honest.
> - How much of it feels owned by staff? How much is still being done to them rather than with them?
> - If you were to redesign your performance management process from scratch, what would you keep? What would you drop?
> - What would happen if you started with MIQs instead of objectives?
> - How comfortable are your leaders with holding reflective, open-ended conversations that are not tied to outcomes?
> - What one small change could you make now that would move your current system closer to one based on growth, motivation and voice?
> - Finally, if your staff were asked what performance management feels like in your setting, what would they say? And what do you want them to say?

Chapter summary

Performance management has long been one of those processes we inherit without question. It's often done to us, not with us – something that lands in our calendars with a meeting and a form, rather than a meaningful sense of purpose. But what I've seen, what I've experienced and what I now know is this: performance management can be so much more. When we reframe it as a tool for growth, as a practice rooted in autonomy, motivation and personal development,

Performance management: A shift worth making

it begins to feel like something we own rather than something we endure.

This chapter has taken you through a journey of what performance management can become when we're brave enough to step outside of tradition. Whether it was through the example of Whitechapel C of E primary school reimagining their approach using MIQs (case study 1), or the work with a CEO who wanted deeper conversations with his executive team (case study 2), the message is clear: change is possible and powerful.

Performance management works best when it's not about ticking boxes but about creating space. Space for reflection. Space for honest dialogue. Space to talk about not only *how* we teach or lead, but *why* we do it. MIQs offered a structured, yet deeply personal, way into these conversations, helping staff and leaders align their daily work with what truly drives them.

Leadership doesn't always mean leading from the front. Sometimes it's about stepping back and creating conditions for others to lead their own development. That's exactly what happened at Whitechapel. The leadership team didn't hold the reins tighter, they let go – and in doing so, they created a culture of ownership, trust and intrinsic motivation. And that's the point. Growth doesn't come from pressure. It comes from purpose.

We can't keep performance management as a standalone process divorced from our values. It must reflect who we are and what we want for our schools. A system that values reflection, not just results. That is shaped by voice, not just policy. That recognises growth as personal, professional and always evolving.

This work is not about abandoning accountability; it's about rebalancing it. Bringing back humanity, purpose and connection into a process that has, for too long, been driven by compliance. When done well, performance management can inspire. It can reignite passion. It can unlock potential. We just have to be willing to do it differently.

Interlude 5
by Andy Buck

> Burton & Buchan (2015) once said: 'There is increasing evidence which demonstrates there's no need to consider the two outcomes independently of each other (engagement and well-being), indeed it is probably detrimental to do so.' This perspective sits at the heart of what leadership consultant Andy Buck (CEO Leadership Matters, author and speaker) shares in the reflection that follows.

Andy's reflection

Culture and climate

What you do as a leader makes a difference to the results you achieve. But the relationship between leadership and results isn't direct. As mentioned later, the actions you take as a leader have a significant impact on the culture and climate within your sphere of influence.

Leadership and results

In this context, *culture* is essentially 'the way we do things around here' and relates to systems, procedures and common practices delivered to a high standard. A useful way of thinking of culture is to consider what someone new joining your team would see happening on a day-to-day basis and the extent to which everyone in the team is working in the same way and to the same level of expectation. Is there a consistent set of high expectations from you about how your team should work? As a result of this, for example, is the early years team you oversee inspiring and well organised? Do the staff in the team have strong and supportive relationships with their peers and all the colleagues they work with?

Climate is more about how it *feels* to work in a team. For your team, this reflects its morale, how appreciated your team feels and the degree of trust within the team as a whole. This is much more difficult to describe or measure, but there is evidence to suggest that the effect of climate on team productivity is considerable.

Discretionary effort

The more positive the culture and climate you create, the more likely your team is to go the extra mile. This concept is known as *discretionary effort*. It commonly describes the input from individuals over and above what is required in their contracts. Critical in this context, however, is that this effort is productive. You will probably know of well-meaning and hard-working colleagues who regrettably did not have the impact their efforts deserved because they were too often not sufficiently focused on the right things.

In other words, it's not about working longer or harder. That can cause stress, burn-out and disaffection which lead to too many people quitting their jobs – an ongoing challenge in our profession. It's about caring about one's work in a way that means individuals are constantly striving to improve, to be a tiny bit better tomorrow than they were yesterday. Getting the culture and climate right can therefore also have an impact on an individual's intention to stay at a place of work, which in turn affects overall retention levels. If you accept the argument that the bigger problem for many schools and trusts is retention, not recruitment, then getting these basic conditions right is crucial for everybody involved.

By creating strong buy-in and engagement, there is no limit on how far you can travel together.

Building discretionary effort

Try to avoid falling into the trap of believing these are all about the warm and fluffy stuff. A great culture includes high expectations combined with appropriate challenge and support.

Greater engagement or discretionary effort doesn't, indeed *shouldn't*, mean that people are working longer and longer hours. It is about people feeling motivated to work more effectively. In fact, if your staff are working longer and longer hours and looking more and more exhausted, this should act as a flag to you that your systems may need a tweak or two.

The Human Side of School Leadership

In conclusion

To return to Burton and Buchan's quote, if we want to build the wellbeing of our staff, it's not about offering yoga on a Thursday after school. It's about creating the culture and climate where engagement is high, where colleagues are healthily challenged and valued, where relationships are seen as central to building discretionary effort. That is the way to build a happy and thriving staff team who are motivated and inspired.

6
Carefrontations
Enabling the hard conversations through psychological safety

> **Connecting question:** When was the last time someone gave you feedback that grew you?

We often avoid the conversations we most need to have. Not because we *don't* care but because we *do*. Conflict is rarely about shouting matches. Most of the time, it's silence. Distance. Avoidance. We tell ourselves it'll sort itself out, or we try to rise above it. But unresolved tension doesn't go away, it festers. And in schools, where relationships are everything, we can't afford to carry that weight around.

Carefrontation is something I've come to use a lot in my own leadership and in the work I do with schools. It's the act of approaching difficulty with care at the centre. It's not about being soft; it's about being human. Mark Finnis, in *Restorative Practice* (2019a), talks about relationships being the heart of restorative practice. If that's true, and I believe it is, then we owe it to each other to be honest in a way that strengthens connection, not breaks it.

The power of carefrontation isn't just internal; it's evidence-based and unapologetically bold. As Lisa Nichols, in *Abundance Now* (2016), puts it, carefrontation is 'the intention of completing the conversation with the relationship still intact'. That's it. That simple. We go into the hard talk not to win or be right but to repair, to connect, to grow together.

Lisa offers a stem phrase that's as clear and powerful as it is kind: 'I want to have a conversation with you that may be difficult for me to say and may be difficult for you to hear. But it's coming from a place of love and respect.'

A phrase such as this changes the tone from confrontation to connection before a single issue is even raised. It holds space for the discomfort while rooting it in care. When I use it, I see shoulders relax. People breathe. They know it's not an attack, it's an offering.

Lisa also suggests a structure, such as the one below.

- **State your intention:** 'What I want to happen in this conversation is that we ...'
- **Affirm the person:** 'What I appreciate about you is ...'
- **Raise the challenge:** 'I need your support in ...'
- **Close with care:** 'So I want to honour you for hearing me out ...'

This doesn't mean the conversation won't be challenging. It just means it won't be destructive. We aren't showing up to dominate we're showing up to reconnect.

To have these conversations, people need to feel safe. Kim Scott's work on *Radical Candor* (2017) reminds us that to challenge well, we have to show we care first. Without care, we drift into ruinous empathy or manipulative insincerity. It's not just about honesty. It's about the courage to care and the care to be courageous.

And we need to model this. As leaders, we don't wait for others to create safety, we set the tone. Whether we're giving feedback or receiving it, addressing harm or naming assumptions, we choose to lead with curiosity rather than control.

What I've learned is that the most powerful carefrontations are the ones that start before the issue. They begin in the culture. In the tone of meetings. In the moments we notice someone withdrawing or stepping back, and we ask not intrusively, but kindly 'How are you, really?' It's about spotting the unsaid before it becomes the unmanageable.

Carefrontation also asks us to examine how we handle emotion – our own and others'. If someone gets upset, our role isn't to shut it down, it's to hold it safely. It's a privilege to be trusted with someone's vulnerability. I often say, you don't have to fix someone's emotion, you just have to honour it. That alone is powerful.

And for those who lead others, this takes intention. It means building enough relational capital that when the difficult moment comes, it's not a shock; it's part of a healthy, open way of working. When we do this well, carefrontations don't become events. They become part of the fabric of our culture.

It's not perfect. I've got it wrong. I've delayed conversations, sugar-coated truths, tried to soften messages that needed more clarity. And each time I've learned that avoiding short-term discomfort almost always creates long-term disconnection.

The best carefrontations I've ever been part of didn't leave people feeling small, they left people feeling seen. And that, in the end, is what makes the difference.

When the system gets in the way – navigating organisational tensions

Sometimes the conflict isn't personal, it's systemic. Policies, expectations and structures that unintentionally create pressure points. A staff member might not be resistant to change, but the way change is communicated feels rushed or impersonal. A middle leader may not lack capability, but they've never had space to practise the leadership being asked of them.

I worked with a MAT where the performance management system was unintentionally creating friction. Targets were set top-down with little conversation and even less alignment with personal goals. The result? Staff who complied but didn't feel connected to the process. Conversations felt like appraisals, not growth. We sat down with the executive team and explored what would happen if we made space for professional storytelling narratives over numbers.

We rewrote the process to include MIQs, reflective prompts and strengths-based goals. And slowly, the energy shifted. Instead of defensive feedback meetings, staff began initiating conversations about their own development. Not because they *had* to but because they *wanted* to.

The Human Side of School Leadership

It's not revolutionary, it's relational

The system must match the culture you're trying to create. If the calendar doesn't make space for reflection, reflection won't happen. If we rush every conversation, we sacrifice depth. Emotional resilience doesn't live in the margins; it's embedded in the systems we build.

Harvard Business Review's (2023) research backs this up. Teams who engage in productive conflict and constructive dialogue backed by a culture of psychological safety consistently outperform teams that don't. But that safety isn't just about tone. It's about clarity. As Susan Scott (2004, 2017) reminds us, the greatest cause of failed relationships comes from unspoken conversations.

I remember being in a school where performance management reviews were scheduled back-to-back in one afternoon. Ten-minute slots. Staff came in with printouts and spreadsheets, a few ticks in boxes, some notes and a nervous smile. It was formal. It was efficient. But it was empty. Not one person left the room feeling seen. There was no room to breathe, let alone reflect. That is the cost of systems that are operationally sound but relationally barren.

On the flip side, I've worked with schools where the system is more agile. Where coaching conversations are timetabled, not optional. Where middle leaders are trained not just in line management but in listening. In these environments, the conversations deepen because people feel safe enough to explore, not just report. They begin to name tensions and offer ideas because they trust they'll be heard. That's what transformation looks like. It's not dramatic. It's consistent. It's woven into the way we meet, how we review, when we check in and what we ask.

We often talk about psychological safety as a climate. But it also needs architecture. It needs us to design with intention. Who sets the agenda for performance reviews? Who holds the power in the conversation? What assumptions are baked into our templates? These things matter. Because the structure signals the values.

I often ask leaders: 'What does your system reward? Is it compliance or curiosity? Is it metrics or meaning?' Because if we say we want reflection but only measure outcomes, we're not aligning *what* we believe with *how* we behave. And people notice that. Systems that reward surface-level reporting end up with surface-level engagement.

In a coaching session with a deputy head, we looked at their school improvement plan. It was detailed, ambitious, tightly worded. But when I asked how it was lived out in staff development conversations, they paused. 'I don't think we really talk about it,' they admitted. That pause told me everything. The document had weight, but no voice. It hadn't translated into dialogue. And that's where systems falter – not in the writing, but in the living.

We have to design systems that invite participation. That make it easy, even expected, for people to share what's working and what isn't. That don't just *allow* for feedback but *welcomes* it. Because the more inclusive your process, the more insightful your progress.

The weight of unspoken tension – why we can't afford to ignore it

One of the most dangerous things in any team is what goes unsaid. The unsaid accumulates. It turns into gossip, disengagement, even attrition. Someone leaves and people say, 'We didn't see it coming', when, in fact the signs were always there. We just weren't listening in the right way.

Unspoken tension isn't always loud. Sometimes it's in the side conversations after meetings, the eye rolls, the absence of ideas from someone who used to contribute more. And in school settings where change is constant and stakes are high, those silences can cost us dearly.

One school I supported had a brilliant deputy who suddenly became quiet during SLT meetings. They weren't disengaged, just quieter. The headteacher assumed it was stress. But when they finally sat down for a real conversation – one rooted in curiosity, not performance – they uncovered that the deputy was holding back because they felt overshadowed. The head had been unknowingly answering every question before the team could even think.

The Human Side of School Leadership

It was a simple shift. The head agreed to ask, pause and wait. Within weeks, the meetings felt different. That deputy stepped back into their space not because they were told to, but because they were invited.

That's what carefrontations offer: the chance to invite people back into the space they belong in.

But that only works when we've built a culture where people believe their voice matters. I've sat in rooms where someone has contributed tentatively, and no one acknowledged it. Not because the idea was poor, but because the room was already onto the next thing. Those moments stay with people. Not being heard is one thing; being ignored is another. The latter leaves a deeper mark.

We need to normalise asking questions such as: 'What *didn't* we talk about today that we should have?' or 'Who h*aven't* we heard from yet?' These aren't just inclusion techniques, they're signals. They show people that silence isn't expected and that everyone has a right to shape the conversation, not just absorb it.

I remember coaching a head who was facing resistance from a senior colleague. Every time they brought up a change, the colleague nodded but then subtly undermined the message with side comments or vague follow-ups. The head wanted to address it but felt unsure how to do so without escalating things. We worked on *naming* the tension, not *accusing*, nor *avoiding*, but *inviting* reflection. They opened the conversation with, 'I've noticed something in our recent exchanges, and I wanted to understand it better rather than assume.' That simple sentence opened the door. The colleague admitted they felt left out of decision-making, and instead of pushing back, the headteacher leaned in. They found a new rhythm, not because one person 'won', but because both felt heard.

Unspoken tension thrives where assumptions live. We assume someone is fine because they're smiling. We assume someone agrees because they're quiet. We assume someone is disengaged when they might actually be disheartened. And the truth is we'll never know unless we ask.

Sometimes staff just need to know they're safe enough to name something awkward. I've heard teaching assistants say: 'I didn't know I was allowed to speak in that meeting.' Not because anyone explicitly said they couldn't but because no one had ever made it feel like they could.

Carefrontations

This is why emotional literacy matters. Not just the words we use, but how we read the room. How we pay attention to body language, hesitations, drop-offs in contribution. Silence speaks. But only if we're trained to hear it.

And for some, especially those with minoritised identities or those who've had difficult past experiences with leadership, that silence is also protection. It's not apathy. It's survival. And until we actively dismantle the reasons that silence feels safer than speech, we won't unlock the full potential of our teams.

In my work, the most transformational moments haven't come from grand strategy; they've come from one brave conversation. One moment where someone said, 'Can I just say something that's been on my mind?' and the room paused, breathed and truly listened.

That is the antidote to unspoken tension. Not more policy. Not more protocol. Just more presence.

Deepening team cohesion through time to think

Conflict doesn't always come from dysfunction. It can arise even in high-functioning, high-performing teams where differences of opinion are strong and deeply held. One SLT I worked with was exactly that. They weren't fractured or combative, but their conversations would often hit a ceiling when assumptions or internal beliefs got in the way.

It wasn't about fixing something broken. It was about helping them move from good to exceptional to create a team culture where difference sparked curiosity, not defensiveness.

We started by introducing individual coaching sessions using Nancy Kline's *Time to Think* (1999) approach. Each leader was given structured space to think aloud, free from interruption, judgement or fixing. Just time. Time to hear themselves. Time to realise which patterns they had been stuck in.

Then we brought it into group facilitation. I created spaces where each voice was truly heard – no jumping in, no premature problem-solving. People spoke with more care, listened more fully, and started to recognise each other's triggers and values. They began to ask: What

The Human Side of School Leadership

might be fueling that reaction? What part of this tension is about the issue and what part is about the fear behind it?

It wasn't therapy. It was leadership. It was professional trust in action. And it moved them from individual performance to shared alignment. One of the leaders said: 'I feel like I've been working with these people for years, but this is the first time I truly understand how they work.' That's the power of depth.

Because when you understand not just *what* someone does, but *why* they do it, you create the conditions to move from collision to cohesion.

This shift didn't happen overnight. It came through disciplined practice embedding intentional silence, resisting the urge to fix and reframing moments of tension as opportunities for insight. The more the group committed to slowing down, the more the quality of their thinking accelerated. It was almost counterintuitive. The less they rushed to resolve, the more deeply they resolved what mattered.

What emerged was a team more attuned not only to each other's roles but to each other's values. A deputy head, who had previously felt sidelined in strategic discussions, shared that they finally felt their voice landed – not just heard but considered. And what changed wasn't their language. It was the space around it. They had room to finish a thought without interruption. That in itself was revolutionary.

We also worked with the idea of assumptions. Every team has them. Stories we tell ourselves about colleagues: 'they always push back', 'they're not strategic', 'they won't get it'. Time to think helped make these stories visible. We weren't naming people; we were naming patterns. That gave us a shared language for accountability without blame.

In one session, I asked the group to finish the sentence, 'One thing I've assumed about someone on this team is ...' followed by, 'One thing I've now learned is ...'. The responses were raw, honest and humanising. There were tears. There was laughter. And, above all, there was a new kind of clarity.

They left that day not just with tools but with a renewed sense of relational safety. A sense that disagreement didn't mean disconnection. That challenge didn't mean threat. It meant we trusted each other enough to stretch. Because high-performing teams don't avoid difference, they learn to dance with it.

And when we get to that place of cohesion, it's not just felt in meetings. It shows up in how feedback is given, how conflict is navigated and how ideas are built not by the loudest voice, but through true collaboration. That's what happens when teams are given the time and the trust to truly think.

Coaching through limiting beliefs and emotional triggers

Conflict doesn't always begin with others; it often begins within. I remember working with a middle leader who was constantly on edge, reading criticism where there was none, always defending before anything was said. It was draining for her and for her team. In our coaching conversations, we traced it back to an early belief that 'being wrong meant being less than'. That was her lens. And once we named it, we could challenge it.

Coaching isn't just about supporting action. It's about gently unpacking the inner narratives that get in our way. The stories we've told ourselves for years about not being good enough, smart enough, ready enough. As a coach and leader, I've learned that the deeper work is often less about solutions and more about permission. Permission to see yourself clearly. To unlearn. To lead from self-awareness rather than self-protection.

When SLTs function from self-awareness, conflict becomes a site of curiosity, not a battlefield. And that's where performance transforms not through metrics, but through mindset.

So much of what we label as 'behaviour' in leadership settings is often the symptom of something deeper unseen and unspoken. I've worked with leaders who came across as abrasive or emotionally distant, only to find that underneath that exterior was a fear of not being respected, of losing credibility, or of being seen as weak. We carry so much that doesn't belong to us. Beliefs inherited from past roles, past teams, even past trauma.

The Human Side of School Leadership

There was one headteacher I coached who carried the burden of always needing to be the one who had the answer. They felt that admitting uncertainty would invite scrutiny or, worse, judgement. In coaching, we slowed everything down. We explored the cost of that belief. How it led to isolation. How it stopped their team from growing because everything came back to them. And slowly, they began to shift. They started saying: 'I don't know yet, but let's think it through together.' It changed everything. Not just for them but for their team.

This work isn't about turning leaders into therapists or softening standards. It's about integrity. It's about congruence. Because when what we feel, say and do are in alignment we create clarity. And clarity is one of the greatest gifts we can offer our teams.

Case study: Working with a CEO – reclaiming depth in executive conversations

Not long ago, I worked with a CEO who led with integrity and vision, but who recognised there was something missing in his executive leadership conversations. 'We talk strategies all day,' he told me, 'but I don't really know what's underneath those ideas for my team'. He wanted depth. Not just alignment, but understanding. And that began with him.

He completed his own set of MIQs first. He reflected on his own experience of leadership, what mattered to him, what frustrated him, and what he hoped to bring into his role that he hadn't yet named aloud. Then we invited his executive team to do the same. Not as an add-on, but as a leadership foundation.

We didn't just fill forms, we had conversations. Brave ones. Honest ones. Ones that surfaced personal values, past hurts and unspoken motivations. We made space for what hadn't been said. It wasn't therapy, but it was healing. And from that, the team started to engage differently. They listened to hear, not to respond. They pushed back with care, not defensiveness. Decisions were still made, but they were made *with* people, not *around* them.

One of the directors said: 'This is the first time I've felt seen and heard without having to prove anything.' That's what carefrontation does. It creates safety not by avoiding conflict but by humanising it.

The CEO reflected afterwards that this work didn't just shift the atmosphere, it sharpened the strategic thinking. With deeper understanding came deeper accountability. People no longer assumed consensus, they earned it. And when challenge arose, it wasn't a surprise. It was welcomed, expected and engaged with openly.

We also explored their limiting assumptions not just about others, but about themselves. What narratives were they carrying into every meeting? What assumptions were being made about capability, resilience or intent? In one session, the CEO admitted, 'I realise I've been holding back on offering opportunities to one team member because I assumed they weren't ready. But I never actually asked.' That moment of awareness became a turning point.

The next step was creating regular rhythm and rituals for these deeper check-ins. Not as one-offs, but as part of how the executive team now functions. Half-termly reflection circles. Pair conversations. Leadership journaling. This wasn't a new initiative; it was an investment in culture.

Because when we build depth into how our teams connect, everything else becomes easier. Feedback lands with less friction. Disagreements are less personal. Trust doesn't have to be rebuilt after every challenge it's already there.

That's the kind of leadership that doesn't just drive performance. It sustains it.

Saying a kind 'No' – boundaries as an act of care

One of the most liberating things we can learn in leadership is how to say 'No' and mean it with kindness. Not as a shutdown, but as a boundary rooted in clarity.

I often support leaders who feel burnt out not because they don't care, but because they care too much and say 'Yes' to everything. Saying 'yes' when your heart is saying 'no' isn't noble; it's a slow form of self-erasure. As author Lisa Nichols (2019) has suggested, the single word 'No' is actually a complete sentence. But I've found a slightly gentler version that still holds the line: 'That's not something I can take on right now, but I appreciate you asking.'

It leaves the door open to respect, while being firm in boundary. Because care isn't about compliance, it's about sustainability.

In performance management, we often associate saying 'no' with resistance or disengagement. But saying 'no' can be the most engaged thing we do when it's done transparently. It makes space for others. It models self-respect. It invites clarity. A kind 'no' honours both the relationship and the reality.

We need to normalise saying 'no' in professional spaces not as defiance, but as design. Leadership isn't about being all things to all people. It's about knowing where you add the most value and being disciplined enough to protect that. I often ask leaders to practise saying 'no' out loud, not to others but to themselves. To the part of themselves that feels guilty, or fears judgement or worries that saying 'no' will somehow diminish their worth.

Boundaries are not barriers; they are clarity – and clarity is kind

I worked with one deputy head who said 'Yes' to every extra duty from last-minute cover to evening events. They were exhausted. When we explored the why, it came down to identity: they felt being helpful was who they were. But being helpful doesn't mean being endlessly available. We reframed helpfulness to include sustainability. They practised saying 'no' with phrases like, 'I can't take that on right now, but can I help you think through who else might support?' It changed everything. Their workload lightened, their confidence grew and others began to step up more.

Carefrontations

Saying 'no' can also be an invitation. An invitation for shared ownership, for creative solutions, for others to grow. When leaders always say 'yes', they unintentionally hoard opportunities. A kind 'no' makes space for others to rise.

Learning how to say 'no' isn't just about boundaries, it's about energy. The kind of energy you bring into the room when you're saying 'yes' out of duty versus saying 'yes' from a place of alignment. One carries a weight. The other creates momentum. And your team can tell the difference.

Saying 'no' also teaches others to trust your 'yes'. If you always agree, your 'yes' loses meaning. But when you say 'yes' from a place of intention and choice, it lands with weight and purpose. Your team knows you've thought it through. That you're all in. That your 'yes' means something. Think back to 'Teach me how to treat you'.

I've worked with leadership teams who've started to bring this into their day-to-day dialogue. One school created a shared language around what they called 'values-based boundaries'. They encouraged staff to name the value behind the 'no'. For example, 'I'm saying "no" because I need to protect my preparation time so I can give my best to my students.' Suddenly, 'no' longer was 'no' a refusal. It became a declaration of purpose.

In the same school, SLT members modelled this openly. They invited others to do the same. And what followed was a deeper respect not just for boundaries, but for the people behind them. The culture shifted. From obligation to ownership. From pleasing to principled. And that's what sustainability looks like.

Saying 'no' is also part of safeguarding wellbeing. Burnout isn't always about volume, it's about values. When we consistently work in ways that betray our values, our energy drains. Saying 'no' is one way to stay aligned. To work in a way that honours both the role and the person within it.

Reflection exercise

Take a look at these questions. Think about your answers. You may find it useful to make a note of them.

- What conversation have you delayed out of fear it may damage a relationship?
- What's your default reaction to conflict: fight, flight, fix or freeze?
- Where might your own limiting beliefs be driving assumptions in your team?
- When was the last time someone gave you feedback that grew you?
- How would your SLT describe the emotional safety in your meetings?
- What can you do to ensure performance isn't prioritised over people?
- Where might a kind 'no' be more honest than a reluctant 'yes'?
- What do your current boundaries say about what you value?
- How are you modelling care through clarity?
- What might become possible if your team embraced brave conversations as standard practice?

Chapter summary

This chapter isn't a one-size-fits-all guide to conflict but an invitation to make conversations count. We've talked about the unsaid, the assumed, the avoided. And through that, we've unpacked how to build cultures where difference isn't feared, it's harnessed.

Restorative practice, emotional intelligence, radical candour ... They aren't just frameworks. They are signals. That who you are matters. That how we show up with each other matters. That listening is leadership.

Harvard Business Review's work on emotional resilience (2021) says this clearly: teams who engage in constructive tension with psychological safety outperform those who don't speak up. It's not just about being nice. It's about being real. And brave. And clear.

Ultimately, your ability to work through conflict defines your ability to lead. It sets the tone. It builds trust. And it invites others to do the same. Saying a kind 'no', hosting brave conversations, dismantling assumptions, and listening not to fix but to understand this is the work. This is what creates cultures of courage. And courage isn't loud. It's consistent.

We create psychologically safe environments when we do the slow work of noticing. Of asking not just '*What* are we doing?' but '*How* are we doing it, and *why*?' When we treat conflict as a mirror, not a monster.

This is about choosing courage over comfort. About daring to name what's not working and being open to hearing what others see that we don't. It's about stepping into conversations with honesty, knowing that clarity is kindness. That feedback is a gift. And that boundaries are an act of leadership.

We've explored how to move beyond avoidance. How to bring emotional honesty into high-stakes spaces. How to create team cultures that don't just survive disagreement but grow from it. Because when we do this well, we don't just improve systems, we transform relationships.

I want to leave you with this: brave spaces are built, not found. They are intentional. And the next time conflict shows up, ask not how to get through it but what it's here to teach.

Interlude 6
by Yamini Bibi

> Fiona Morris, a school leader, once said, 'Feedback is a gift.' This perspective sits at the heart of what education consultant and coach Yamini Bibi (CDP trainer, consultant and speaker) shares in the reflection that follows.

Yamini's reflection

When I became a Lead Practitioner in a school in East London, one of the deputy headteachers, Fiona Morris, would always say 'feedback is a gift'. At the time, it was my first middle leadership role and I did not really understand its significance. However, as I have moved through my career, this is the one quote that I return to time and again.

Why feed back when talking about culture and wellbeing? I think feedback, whether positive or challenging, is a central part of any role in any organisation; without it we feel uncertain, misunderstood, disempowered, devalued and this can lead to people leaving organisations as a result.

I have to admit that in my initial middle and senior leadership roles, giving feedback to those I line managed and supported was a struggle. I am a self-proclaimed people pleaser and I thought that by giving feedback to someone, it would harm the way they viewed me and my relationship with them. Interestingly, I was able to give feedback about lesson observations because, in my mind, I was helping them to improve their classroom practice and in turn helping young people thrive academically. However, I could not apply this same idea as a leader. Now, as a former experienced senior leader and consultant, I understand why feedback that

Interlude 6

provides high challenge alongside high support is crucial to others feeling successful in their roles. When people feel successful within the school environment, they tend to feel more positive and optimistic and valued. Most people prefer to receive feedback in an open and transparent manner.

It has taken me years of reading about effective feedback and attending different leadership courses to understand how I might give feedback effectively so that I can provide support while also stretching people I lead. Dr Jaz Ampaw-Farr, author and international speaker, in her Humans First Leadership course, helped me to reframe feedback as 'fighting for the highest possible good of those we lead'. If we are always aiming to fight for others to be the best they can be, then feedback is necessary. It is, after all, the kind thing to do to inform someone openly and transparently if they are doing something well or if they could improve in an aspect of their practice.

I have been very lucky to work with headteachers like Thahmina Begum from Community Schools Trust, where I observed how feedback really can be a gift when it is clear, specific and measurable. Thahmina used frameworks for giving feedback to train us as leaders which I still use regularly. When receiving feedback from Thahmina, I never felt upset or defensive because I knew it always came from a place of care. If we want staff to feel valued and cared for, leaders need to be explicitly trained on how to give feedback because it can then create a culture of support and empowerment.

I believe it is therefore the kind approach to see feedback as a gift because we are empowering others to thrive and 'fighting for the highest possible good' of those we lead, which in turn will create a culture of wellbeing in any organisation.

7
Headteachers
How to care for yourself when you're responsible for the welfare of all

> **Connecting question:** Have you felt lonely in your role and what has helped you feel more connected?

The quiet weight of leadership

I've been there. In your position. The responsibility, the loneliness. The 'I have to carry it all' and show no vulnerability. Now we hear how we *should* be vulnerable, the opening this provides for others to be open. Sometimes that creates more anxiety than it alleviates. The dissonance of showing vulnerability and not appearing weak. Maintaining professionalism and personal integrity while keeping the faith of staff in your leadership.

It's a strange paradox. We tell ourselves we must show strength, but we are quietly exhausted. We are told to model vulnerability, but we fear being misunderstood. That inner conflict plays out quietly but constantly in our bodies, in our decision-making, in our relationships with our staff and governors. Vulnerability is not a strategy; it's a practice, and it's not always safe to practise it in every room. So we learn to carry that emotional duality. We smile while aching. We reassure others while questioning ourselves. It's a tension few talk about but many live with daily.

The Human Side of School Leadership

Beneath the titles

'Who are you beneath your titles?' is a question I often ask leaders and one we have previously explored. Breaking down the titles and roles we assimilate and hold onto as our identity becomes morphed into the functions we carry out. Leaders have an air of mystery about them. No longer in the teacher camp, they maintain strict boundaries often appearing isolated and distant. But does it have to be this way? We are built to connect with the people we work with. We silently move into the ranks of leadership leaving the very personal relationships we have built over time somewhat behind us.

There's often no rite of passage, no one moment that declares 'You are now a leader'. Instead, it creeps up. A few more responsibilities. A new title. Suddenly, you're in rooms you never expected to be in, making decisions that ripple across dozens or hundreds of lives. The identity shift is real. And if we're not careful, it consumes us. We become the title. We live the role. But inside, we're still figuring it out. The person behind the leader remains largely unseen – sometimes even to ourselves.

Models of leadership that reflect the real

We have a suite of nationally recognised leadership courses and models of leaders we have experienced which further reinforce our sense of having to hold it all together. Where are the real models of leadership, the messiness and understanding that we are not and will never be perfect? The strive for the perfect leader with no chinks in their armour? A leader who looks after everyone else and holds their life together perfectly? The swan-like pose and posture?

Leadership isn't about perfection. It's about honesty. Integrity. The willingness to own the parts we're still learning. It's about staying in dialogue with ourselves and others even when it's uncomfortable. I've seen more transformation happen in leaders who say, 'I'm struggling with this' than in those who act as though everything is fine. Staff don't need superheroes. They need humans who lead with courage and clarity. That's real leadership. The kind that allows others to be more of themselves too.

The models we've inherited often celebrate control, composure and relentless drive. But we need more models that show what it looks like to pause. To seek help. To set boundaries. To rest. Because when leaders do that, they give others permission to do the same.

Support structures that truly support

Headteachers are often everything to everyone and no one to themselves. Do the mechanisms of true support for the senior leader exist? And by mechanisms I am talking about protected time to receive coaching and/or supervision. To carve out time to think so that you can lead effectively. Leading from a position of clarity and care for yourself first. Not a selfish act but an act of self-care. Not a *should* but a *must* (yes, it's the DfE language here). I'm waiting for when wellbeing support for headteachers becomes a statutory requirement.

Let's be honest: too many headteachers are working in survival mode. They're holding the emotional climate of the entire school without anyone holding theirs. That's not sustainable. Coaching, supervision, reflective time – these aren't luxuries; they're essentials. They're the difference between reacting and responding, between fatigue and foresight.

I've worked with heads who told me they hadn't had a space to talk honestly in years. Not because they didn't want to but because there was never time. Or the fear of being judged. Or the belief that everyone else was coping better. But once they had the space, coaching, time to think, a confidential reflective session, the relief was palpable. It was like letting go of a breath they didn't know they were holding.

And let's name the bigger truth: when leaders are well, schools are well. When leaders feel supported, they lead from vision, not survival. They communicate with care, not defensiveness. They model balance, not burnout. The ripple effects are real and tangible. Staff notice. Children benefit. Culture shifts.

The Human Side of School Leadership

So yes, I am calling for statutory wellbeing support for school leaders. But more than that, I'm calling for a shift in culture. A culture where we no longer celebrate exhaustion as evidence of commitment. Where rest is seen as preparation, not laziness. Where support is proactive, not reactive. And where every leader knows: you matter too.

Values in action

A practice that I like to hold with leaders is asking them about the values they hold. A straightforward question you would say. I normally receive answers such as 'kind', 'compassionate', 'driven', 'selfless' and so on. I follow by asking them whether their values are received in that way. This is when we become a little bit unstuck and uncomfortable. You can say that you feel you are the type of leader who is, but how is that received by others? Where is the evidence? And why shouldn't we ask and not wait for a 360 diagnostic tell us how a chosen few perceive us. I often ask heads/principals to do away with the first agenda item and hold onto connectedness, asking others how they feel you show your values, and then vice versa. Opening up the floodgates to truly talk about how you are with each other and how you hold yourself.

It is one thing to declare our values but another entirely to embody them in spaces where tension or pressure runs high. Values are not what we write on the wall or list in a CPD session. They show up in how we respond when we're interrupted, how we handle disagreement, how we hold boundaries and how we make people feel in our presence. That's why asking SLT members to reflect on how they experience each other's values is so powerful. It isn't a tickbox exercise. It's a mirror.

One executive principal did just this after our session together. He held an SLT meeting and asked his team whether they genuinely felt his values in the way he led and interacted with them. The openness this single, courageous question brought into the room created just the type of raw honesty that was so needed. He received different perspectives honest, varied and heartfelt. Each one was something he deeply valued and many offered insights he hadn't previously considered. What struck him most was something profoundly human: his team expressed a strong desire to look after him, just as he consistently looked after them. This moment of shared vulnerability and reflection shifted the dynamic not just between him and his team, but across the whole leadership group. It reminded everyone that leadership is not a solitary performance, but a relational act built on mutual care and trust.

That moment became a pivot. His team began to speak with more intention and listen with more care. Because now they weren't just working *beside* each other, they were working in *alignment* with shared values they had named, questioned and reflected back to each other. There was trust – not the performative kind, but the kind that's built through truth-telling. This is how values move from being words to being lived.

And it starts with a simple, brave question: How do others experience me?

> **Reflection exercise**
>
> Take the time to think about how others experience you. What is your frame of reference in determining this? Are you values evident? And would your colleagues and teams say they are?

Guilt

Sometimes there is nothing more debilitating than guilt. We carry this weight around with us daily. Its noise a reminder of who we haven't given our best to. Who has only had a smidgen of our time. Who received our frustration or lack of patience. Guilt sets the tone for negative thoughts. It's the strive for something disguised as perfection. So many leaders I support talk about guilt of not being good enough, available enough, a better parent and partner. We are taught to juggle it all and look happy doing it. Where is the fun in that. We would rather pretend than say it as it is. We are not perfect. We are not without flaws. I wondered what it would be like to lead without guilt? How would that free your thinking? How would you feel?

The Human Side of School Leadership

Guilt, for many of us, operates like a constant background hum, a low-level vibration that we've grown so used to, we barely notice how much it shapes us. It doesn't shout, but it tugs. It tugs at your energy, your joy and your self-worth. It's there in the moment you realise you missed your child's assembly. In the realisation that you were present in a meeting but absent in your thoughts when someone needed your attention. It shows up when your phone buzzes during dinner and you look away from your family again. It whispers, 'You should be doing more.'

The pressure to get everything right all the time is immense. Especially for those in leadership where the myth of the endlessly capable, endlessly giving, leader persists. But guilt doesn't make us better. It makes us smaller. It narrows our view and traps us in the impossible pursuit of proving our worth through over-functioning. And yet, so many of us try. We try to be exceptional at everything and everyone to everybody. It's exhausting. And unsustainable.

Sometimes we confuse guilt with care. We think guilt means we care deeply. And yes, guilt can be a signal, but it shouldn't be a script. It's not the story we need to live by. What would it look like to rewrite that script? What if we could name our limits without shame? What if we gave ourselves the same compassion we so freely give to others? What if we could say, 'I missed the mark today' and let that be a point of reflection, not self-punishment?

When I ask leaders to explore the idea of leading without guilt, the silence is often deafening. It's hard to even imagine. But slowly, we start to uncover what it would mean. It would mean trusting that our value isn't measured in hours worked or emails answered. It would mean knowing that presence matters more than perfection. It would mean believing that you can be a good leader, parent and partner even when you miss a beat.

Guilt loses its grip when we speak it aloud. When we say, 'This is hard' and someone nods in understanding. When we admit that we've shouted at the wrong time, missed something important or simply run out of steam. There's liberation in honesty. And there's power in refusing to let guilt define the kind of leader or person you are.

Headteachers

So, I ask again: What would it be like to lead without guilt? To choose enoughness over endlessness? To show up as you are, not despite your imperfections, but with them? Because maybe the most powerful thing you can do isn't to hide the guilt, but to step out from under it, and lead anyway.

Enoughness over exhaustion

Burnout is often seen as something that happens when we've simply done too much. But I've come to learn it's also about what we haven't done enough of. Rest. Reflection. Saying 'no'. Naming our needs. Being honest. Especially in leadership, burnout doesn't always look like collapsing at your desk; it looks like quiet depletion, slow detachment, joylessness disguised as efficiency.

I sit with leaders who are burnt out but still smiling. Still producing. Still showing up. But inside, they're running on fumes. They tell me they feel guilty for even admitting they're tired, like they're letting someone down by having limits. But we are not robots. We were never meant to lead at the cost of our health.

Brené Brown in *The Gifts of Imperfection* (2018b, 56) reminds us that perfectionism is not the path to excellence. It's a shield. And that shield gets heavy. She writes: 'Perfectionism is a self-destructive and addictive belief system that fuels this primary thought: If I look perfect and do everything perfectly, I can avoid or minimize the painful feelings of shame, judgment, and blame.'

This belief keeps so many leaders stuck. Constantly striving. Never arriving. But the cost is high. Because when you lead from depletion, you lead from defensiveness. Your empathy wears thin. Your creativity dims. Your ability to hold others falters.

So, what would enoughness look like? It's not laziness. It's presence. It's integrity. It's choosing to trust that doing your best does not mean doing it all. It's valuing depth over breadth. It's the courage to say, 'I need a pause', and not apologise for it.

Burnout prevention isn't just personal, it's cultural. If your leadership culture only celebrates those who burn the candle at both ends, it's time to light a new flame. We need to celebrate pacing, boundaries, recovery. We need to make space for leaders to breathe. Not once a year on a retreat but every week, in small, meaningful moments that reconnect them to their why.

You're allowed to rest. And rest isn't the opposite of productivity; it's the foundation of it. A well-rested leader is a present leader. A regulated leader. A human one.

A practical guide to looking after yourself (without the fluff)

I've sat in countless leadership development sessions that tell you to eat well, get more sleep and drink water as if you haven't figured that part out already. What we need is not more generic wellness tips. We need reminders that respect our reality. So, here's a simple, grounded guide that I use with leaders – real strategies, not patronising ones.

1. **Protect your calendar like it's your energy budget:** Don't just book in meetings and performance reviews. Schedule your thinking time. Put in breathing space between emotionally heavy meetings. Block off 20 minutes to eat properly without being on your phone. If you don't claim that time, someone else will.
2. **Start and end the week with intention:** Begin your week asking: 'What will make this week feel purposeful, not just productive?' End the week with: 'What did I learn about myself and others?' It helps to mark your rhythm. It gives you back some agency.
3. **Have one conversation each week where you say what's true:** This could be admitting to your SLT that you're tired. Telling your PA you need time protected. Letting a colleague know you appreciated their feedback, but it landed a bit hard. One honest moment helps restore your equilibrium.
4. **Ask yourself: 'What is mine to carry?':** Sometimes we hold everything. But not everything is ours. Emotional labour, other people's expectations, guilt that's not grounded in fact. Learn to check in: what's mine and what can I set down?

Headteachers

5. **Surround yourself with truth-tellers, not just cheerleaders:** You need people who will ask how you are and wait for the real answer. Build relationships where care and challenge go hand in hand. That kind of circle helps you stay anchored.
6. **Celebrate what you did, not just what's left to do:** Write it down. Speak it aloud. The brain needs small wins. You don't have to wait until a half-term break to validate your effort.

These aren't quick fixes. But they are reminders that you matter, too. That looking after yourself isn't indulgent, it's responsible. Because if you're not well, your leadership can't be either.

Finding self-efficacy: Redefining your role on your own terms

There comes a moment, quiet, but clear, where you realise you're waiting for someone else to give you permission to lead the way you want to. And that moment can be a turning point. Because self-efficacy doesn't arrive through another course or a new initiative. It comes when you stop asking who you need to become and start asking, 'What do I already know about what matters to me in this role?'

I often say to leaders I work with: If you could shape your job to reflect your values, your strengths and the kind of impact you want to have, what would it look like? What would your days feel like? And what's stopping you from inching closer to that?

This isn't about overhauling everything or tearing up your responsibilities. It's about shifting your stance. It's about deciding where you place your energy. Reclaiming agency over your time, your meetings, your calendar and, most of all, your presence.

I've seen leaders waiting for a better structure, more support, the right context. And while those things absolutely help, the truth is that the shift starts with a quiet decision to lead yourself first. To step out of autopilot. To reflect more deliberately. To stop being led by what the system expects and start aligning with what you believe in.

Sometimes this means doing the uncomfortable thing: saying 'no' to something that doesn't align. Sometimes it's asking to do something differently because the current way is draining your spark. And often, it's simply starting with a decision: I am allowed to shape this role to reflect who I am, not just the version I think others expect me to be.

Self-efficacy doesn't mean you never struggle; it means you trust yourself to figure things out. It's not confidence in the sense of bravado; it's quiet self-trust. And that changes how you show up. You stop performing. You start leading.

So, ask yourself: What do I want this role to feel like? What am I allowed to define for myself? And what is one small change I can make this week that brings me closer to that version?

Engaging in wellbeing coaching

Most of my work involves wellbeing coaching/supervision. The primary aim of each session is to hold time for each leader to offload. A precious time for leaders to pose questions, issues, talk it out or even cry it out. An independent, objective and confidential space. If only this offer was mandatory. Each leader deserving of the time to feel heard and supported. Often the only space to feel truly seen, warts and all. Here the mask can slip, the armour can be taken off. The need to hold it together slowly comes away. The pressure slightly relieved.

There's something sacred about this space. Not dramatic or performative, just real. It's quiet. Intentional. It asks nothing of you other than to be. And that is profound. Because so much of leadership asks for output. Impact. Solutions. In wellbeing coaching, the currency is presence. Not fixing, not problem-solving, but being with what is. Naming it. Exploring it. Sitting with discomfort until it begins to soften. This kind of space is rare in education. It shouldn't be.

The power in these sessions comes not from giving advice, but from listening deeply. Reflecting the things leaders often don't realise they've said. Mirroring their values, their pain points, their blind spots. It's not therapy, but it's deeply therapeutic. Not mentoring, but developmental. The blend is what makes it powerful responsive, human and tailored.

Through coaching, I've seen leaders come to see patterns they hadn't noticed – ways they defer to others too quickly or shoulder too much without question. They begin to unpick inherited narratives: 'I must be strong', 'I mustn't let anyone see I'm struggling', 'Everyone else comes first'. Slowly, those beliefs begin to loosen. Not dismissed – but examined. Questioned. Reframed.

Wellbeing coaching helps to reconnect people with their 'why.' It helps you hear your own voice again. When the noise of targets, demands and stretched capacity becomes too loud, coaching brings you back. Back to your intentions, your values, your humanity. It reminds you that before the strategy, before the decisions, you are a person. A person who deserves to be well.

It's also a space where the invisible labour gets named. The emotional load that doesn't show on a spreadsheet. The toll of being the container for everyone else's worries. The countless micro-decisions made every hour. The grief of change. The heartbreak of watching a struggling colleague, a disappointed student or your own child waiting for your attention. These aren't small things. And they deserve to be witnessed.

I often describe coaching as creating a gentle interruption in the noise. A pause. A mirror. A recalibration. It's not about erasing the pressure but changing your relationship with it. Leaders come into sessions tense, guarded and leave just that bit lighter. Seen. Not judged. Affirmed. Not indulged. Held not fixed.

Here's what coaching can offer

- **Clarity:** When everything feels overwhelming, coaching helps you sift through the noise. What's urgent, what's important, what can wait and what isn't yours to carry.
- **Reflection:** It gives you time to think, uninterrupted. A rare luxury in school life. But one that shifts reactive leadership into intentional leadership.
- **Challenge:** It's not always soft. Sometimes coaching means holding up the mirror and asking, 'Is this serving you? Is this true?' That's where the growth happens.
- **Compassion:** The kind that reminds you you're human. That you matter. That tending to your needs isn't weakness, it's wisdom.

The Human Side of School Leadership

One headteacher told me: 'I didn't realise how much I was holding until I let myself say it out loud.' That moment, that release, is everything. Not because everything is solved, but because it's shared.

If I could make this a mandatory offer for every leader, I would. Not as a reactive measure, but as a proactive way of sustaining the people who hold so much. Because when we support our leaders to be well, they lead from a place of presence, empathy and courage.

I've come to believe wellbeing coaching should sit alongside safeguarding and CPD not as an optional extra, but as essential infrastructure. It is protective. Preventative. Restorative. And it signals that we value the person behind the position. That we care enough not just to ask, 'How are you?' but to really make time to hear the answer.

So if you haven't yet experienced this kind of space, seek it. Advocate for it. Reach out. Or create it for someone else. Because everyone deserves a place to take the mask off, drop the performance and just be.

That's where the real work begins.

Example session

So what does a typical session look like? It varies depending on the person, but it always begins with space. We don't dive in; we land. I often begin with a simple question: *What's your story of origin?* Not the version you give your team, but the truth beneath that. From there, we unpick. Sometimes the questions are practical: *What's draining your energy? Where are you holding too much?* Other times they're more reflective: *What needs to be named today? What are you avoiding?* And sometimes, I'll ask: *What would it look like if you led from enough, not guilt?*

They're not fluffy questions. They're real. They demand presence. And they shift people. Because in leadership, no one really asks you those things without wanting something in return. In coaching, the ask is for honesty and the gift is perspective.

Testimonials speak for themselves

'I didn't expect to cry within five minutes. But I also didn't expect to laugh and feel lighter by the end. This space gave me back something I didn't know I had lost myself.'

'You asked me one question that I've carried for months since: "Is this still working for you?" It changed everything.'

'This is the only hour where I don't have to be anyone for anyone else. Just me. That's rare. That's gold.'

Alongside coaching, my work expands into wider offers: keynote speaking for conferences and leadership events, INSET and CPD on *Culture, Care and Connection*, a deeply practical and personal session that helps teams realign not just what they do, but how they do it. I also offer strategic audits to help schools assess the alignment between values and practice. Because wellbeing isn't just personal, it's systemic. We need systems that support what we say we care about.

The work I do is always underpinned by the same principles: listen deeply, challenge kindly and always put the human first. Whether I'm sitting one-to-one with a leader in coaching, working with a whole trust on culture transformation or delivering a keynote to 300 leaders, the message is the same: you matter. Who you are shapes how you lead. And we need you well.

This isn't soft work. It's the most important work. Because if we want education to thrive, we need our leaders to feel whole, not just held together. We need to stop surviving leadership and start living it.

Let this be your invitation: because this is where real leadership begins. You first!

A personal offer to you

As a gesture of care and commitment to the leaders who've taken the time to read this book to really sit with the truths and the discomfort and to stay open, I want to offer you something real and tangible. Every leader who picks up this book, who connects with its words, its

The Human Side of School Leadership

challenges and its invitations, is entitled to a free wellbeing supervision session with me.

Why? Because my mission has never been just about writing or speaking; it's about walking alongside leaders. It's about creating space to think, feel, release and reimagine. I know what it means to be carrying so much with so little space to put it down. This offer isn't a marketing tool; it's a commitment. A chance to land, even for a moment, in a space that's just for you.

This session won't be filled with fluffy platitudes or surface-level coaching. It will be real. Grounded. Just like this book. You'll be met with honesty, confidentiality, care and challenge. The same values I've brought to every chapter, I will bring into that space with you.

If something in this book has resonated, if a sentence made you pause or a question stayed with you, then take the next step. Reach out. You don't have to carry it all alone. And you were never meant to.

To access your free session and speak to a human, not a bot, email info@balance-ed.co.uk

Consider it a small part of the bigger message: you matter, your wellbeing matters, and you do not have to wait until you're at breaking point to feel seen.

Interlude 7
by Bushra Nasir

> Bushra Nasir's mum used an Islamic term when discussing what role we play in life and leadership; she once said, 'Ibadah'. This perspective sits at the heart of what Bushra Nasir (CBE and retired CEO and Deputy Lord Lieutenant of Greater London) shares in the reflection that follows.

Bushra's reflection

This Islamic term 'Ibadah' translates generally into 'worship' or 'servitude' and signifies an act of devotion, obedience, submission to the Almighty. It encompasses all actions intentions and thoughts performed to please the Almighty. Ibadah includes both obligatory rituals like prayer, fasting, Hajj (pilgrimage) and Zakat (charity) as well as good deeds done with sincerity and for the sake of humanity for the sake of the Almighty.

It was a term used by my mother about teaching and that is why this word has influenced my leadership style. She used to say that teaching changes the lives of children, so it is a form of Ibadah. When I was a young teacher, trying to be a full-time teacher, a mother of three children and helping my husband set up his business, she was my greatest supporter and helped me to see my teaching not just as a job but as an honour and a privilege by referring to it as Ibadah. My mother was not allowed to stay on at school after the age of ten. It was considered that she had learned to read and write, and this was all the education that she needed. She was passionate about education and wanted her daughters as well as her sons to go to university and be successful in their careers.

The Human Side of School Leadership

When we teach, lead schools or lead multi-academy trusts, I believe we serve the children, the parents and the communities and change lives. The satisfaction you gain as a teacher and as a leader is seeing the changes with your own eyes but also the belief that your hard work and commitment will be accepted by your Maker, for which you will be rewarded in the Hereafter. I had the privilege of leading Plashet School as a headteacher for 20 years, a multi-religious state school with a majority of Muslim students. I was one of the first female Muslim headteachers in the country and this placed an honour and a privilege on my shoulders as well as a great responsibility. I wanted to ensure that all the girls who attended Plashet School had a positive role model to inspire them and for the parents and the community to see a successful Muslim woman who was an effective leader and who also understood the community needs and challenges. I felt my job was serving the community and the girls of Plashet School, and changing the aspirations and the hopes and dreams of the young women for whom I had responsibility. When I became a CEO of a group of five schools in a predominately white working-class area, my servant leadership style was just as important. Bringing five schools together in one unit, line managing the headteachers and the executive team, as well as assisting the raising of aspirations of the students from backgrounds where education was not valued, required all my experience in servant leadership. Compassion, character and competence allowed me to help build trust with the staff, students and the parents which led to the building of a respected Trust in the middle of a major council estate and our first students going to the Oxbridge and Russell group of universities.

The reward of my 50 years' service in education is helping to change the lives of many young people and their communities and the belief that my mother's constant use of the term 'Ibadah' helped shape my leadership journey.

Final reflections

I wrote this book not to be right, but to be real. To bring a different kind of language into leadership – one rooted in truth, care and courage. Because if we are to create lasting change in our schools, our systems and in ourselves, we need more than strategies. We need soul. We need leaders who are human first, who know the cost of silence, the power of listening and the beauty of connection. This book is my offering, my legacy of sorts. Not because I have the answers, but because I've walked beside too many brilliant people who didn't feel seen in their brilliance. And that must change.

It is written in the legacy of every leader and teacher who simply puts their all into it quietly, consistently, often without thanks, but always with heart. It is also for my late husband, who held an unconditional regard unlike anything I have ever witnessed. His belief in people was unwavering, his care effortless. And it is for my future legacy my grandson Isaac – who I hope will continue the work of guiding by light, by example, and by care. Because this is what the work demands. And it's what the world needs.

So, as you close these pages, I ask you to carry something forward. Not a checklist. Not another initiative. But a promise to yourself to stay close to your values, your voice and your wellbeing. Because when you lead from that place you don't just impact others, you change the culture around you. And that, quietly and powerfully, is how legacy is made. Not in grand moments, but in daily acts of presence, honesty and care. Keep going. We need you well.

References

Amrein-Beardsley, A. (2014). *Rethinking value-added models in education: Critical perspectives on tests and assessment-based accountability.* Harvard Education Press.

Armstrong, M. (2017). *Armstrong's handbook of performance management: An evidence-based guide to delivering high performance* (6th edn; page no. not available). Kogan Page.

Brooks, A. C. (2023). *From strength to strength: Finding success, happiness, and deep purpose in the second half of life.* Penguin Random House.

Brown, B. (2018a). *Dare to lead: Brave work. Tough conversations. Whole hearts.* Random House.

Brown, B. (2018b). *The gifts of imperfection: Let go of who you think you're supposed to be and embrace who you are.* Hazeldon FIRM.

Browne, A. (2021). 'Nothing without us.' Podcast. Angie Browne Coaching.

Buckingham, M. and Goodall, A. (2019). *Nine lies about work: A freethinking leader's guide to the real world.* Harvard Business Review Press.

Burton, J. and Buchan, H. (2015). *Employee engagement and wellbeing: The evidence base.* Chartered Institute of Personnel and Development (CIPD).

Chance UK (no date). F F L Education data lab. Available at: www.chanceuk.com/wp-content/uploads/2024/04/Too-Young-to-Leave-Behind-exec-summary_FINAL-3.pdf (accessed 18 November 2025).

Clear, J. (2018). *Atomic habits: An easy & proven way to build good habits & break bad ones.* Penguin Random House.

Covey, S. R. (1989). *The 7 habits of highly effective people* (page no. not available). Simon & Schuster.

Cuddy, A. J. C., Kohut, M. and Neffinger, J. (2013). Connect, then lead. *Harvard Business Review,* 91(7/8), 54–61.

deNisi, A. and Murphy, K. R. (2017). Performance appraisal and performance management: 100 years of progress? *Journal of Applied Psychology,* 102(3), 421–433.

References

Eastwood, O. (2021). *Belonging: The ancient code of togetherness*. Hachette UK.

Edmondson, A. (2019). *The fearless organization: Creating psychological safety in the workplace for learning, innovation, and growth*. Wiley.

Finnis, M. (2019). *Restorative practice: Building relationships, improving behaviour and creating positive cultures in schools*. Independent Thinking Press.

Gallo, A. (2023). What is psychological safety? *Harvard Business Review*. Available at: https://hbr.org/2023/02/what-is-psychological-safety (accessed 18 November 2025).

Gilligan, C. (1982). *In a different voice: Psychological theory and women's development*. Harvard University Press.

Greenleaf, R. K. (1977). *Servant leadership: A journey into the nature of legitimate power and greatness*. Paulist Press.

Harter, J. K. and Schmidt, F. L. et al. (2020). The relationship between engagement at work and organizational outcomes. 10th edn. Gallup. Available at: https://media-01.imu.nl/storage/happyholics.com/6345/gallup-2020-q12-meta-analysis.pdf (accessed 18 November 2025).

Harvard Business Review (2020). *Emotional resilience in leadership: How teams thrive through challenge*. Harvard Business Publishing.

Harvard Business Review (2017). HBR's 10 must reads on Emotional Intelligence. Harvard Business Review Press.

Kline, N. (1999). *Time to think: Listening to ignite the human mind*. Cassell.

Kline, N. (2020). *The promise that changes everything: I won't interrupt you*. Penguin Life.

Kuvaas, B. (2011). The interactive role of performance appraisal reactions and regular feedback. *Journal of Managerial Psychology*, 26(2), 123–137.

Lakhiani, V. (2016). *The code of the extraordinary mind*. Rodale Books.

Malcolm X. (1964). Speech at Oxford Union, December 3, 1964. Oxford Union Society.

Nichols, L. (2011). *No matter what: 9 steps to living the life you love*. Grand Central Life & Style.

Nichols, L. (2016). *Abundance now* (page nos not available). Dey Street Books.

Schein, E. H. (2017). Culture and leadership in *Organizational culture and leadership*, The Jossey–Bass Business & Management Series.

Scott, K. (2017). *Radical candor: Be a kick-ass boss without losing your humanity*. St. Martin's Press.

Scott, S. (2004). *Fierce conversations: Achieving success at work and in life, one conversation at a time*. Penguin.

Scott, S. (2017). *Fierce conversations: Achieving success at work and in life, one conversation at a time* (3rd edn). Currency.

Shetty, J. (2020). *Think like a monk: Train your mind for peace and purpose every day*. HarperCollins.

References

Sinek, S. (2009). *Start with why: How great leaders inspire everyone to take action.* Portfolio.

Spreitzer, G. and Porath, C. (2012). Creating sustainable performance. *Harvard Business Review*, 90(1/2), 92–99.

Swart, T. (2025). *'4 brain hacks to manifest anything into your life (Science-Backed Method!)*. Podcast.

Syed, M. (2019). *Rebel ideas: The power of diverse thinking.* John Murray Publishers Ltd.

Teacher Wellbeing Index (2023). *Education support.* Available at: www.educationsupport.org.uk (accessed 4 November 2025).

The Co-operative Group (2022). *Community wellbeing index.* The Co-operative Group.

Whetten, D. A. and Cameron, K. S. (2016). *Developing management skills* (9th edn). Pearson.

Index

accountability 71–2, 92; performance management 65–7, 71–2, 77, 79, 81
active listening 61
acts of regard 34–5
acts of service 31
adversity 2
affirmation 16, 31, 33, 86
alignment 107
Ampaw-Farr, Jaz 101
Amrein-Beardsley, A. 69
appraisal 41, 68, 76, 87
Arabic culture: friendship, 12 stages of 6
Armstrong, M. 65, 68
assumptions 92
authenticity *x*, 25, 71
autonomy 32, 71–2, 80

balance *see* work/life balance
Balance:ed 6, 35, 40, 55; aims and objectives 6–7
Begum, Thahmina 101
behaviour 93
belonging *x*, *xii*, 18, 20, 25, 32, 45, 50, 60; performance and 18–19
bias, role of 68
Bibi, Yamini 100–1
blindness *see* perspective blindness
body language 91
boundary-setting 35, 95–7, 105; values-based boundaries 97
Brooks, A. C. 18
Brown, B. 109
Browne, A. 63
Buchan, H. 82, 84

Buck, Andy 82–4
Buddhism: *cancers of the mind* 17–18, 20
burnout *x*, 69, 96, 105, 109–10
Burton, J. 82, 84

care 52, 116; boundary-setting 95–7; connection and culture 15–27
carefrontation *ix*, 85–99; concept of *xii-xiii*
CEOs 63, 94–5, 118; executive conversations 94–5; executive team reflection 78–9
challenge 113, 116
Chance UK 4
Chief Engagement Officers 33
Chief Executive Officers 33
children's services 3
clarity *xiii*, 92, 94–8, 105, 113
Clear, J. 46
climate, defining 82
Co-operative Group 23
coaching 2, 93–4; benefits of 113; typical sessions 114; wellbeing 112–14
colleagues: draining 35–7; uplifting 35–6
collective identity 12
Community Schools Trust 101
comparing *x*, 27
compassion 113, 118
complaining *x*, 27
compliance *ix*, 66–7; compliance-focused performance management *xi*; growth and 69–70; *Whitechapel* case study 40–3

123

Index

confidentiality 59, 116
conflict 85, 87; personal 93; productive 88; resolution *xiii*
connectedness 18
connecting questions 49–61, 85, 103; check-ins 52–3; transformative 53–4
connection *x*, 6, 52; care and culture 15–27; conversations 32–3; psychological safety 21–2, 50–1; staff meetings *xi*; *Whitechapel* case study 40–3
contentment 13
contribution 74–5
conversations 32–3
cortisol 33
courage *xiii*, 86, 99, 104
courageous conversations *xiii*
Covey, S. R. 28, 47
CPD (continuing professional development) 20, 22, 106, 114–15
criticising *x*, 27
Cuddy, A. J. C. 25
cultivation 12
culture 52; care and connection 15–27; climate and 82
curiosity 54–5, 59, 89, 91

deep relationships, importance of forging 49–50
deNisi, A. 67, 68
Department for Education (DfE) 17, 105
discretionary effort 83
disengagement 89

Eastwood, O. 18–19, 24
ECTs (Early Career Teachers) 41
Elevate Trust 47
emotional intelligence *ix*, 39, 98
emotional labour 110
emotional literacy 91
emotional resilience 99
emotional triggers 93–4
empathy *x*, *xiii*, 28, 58–9, 61
empowerment 101
encouragement 31, 37, 54
engagement 50
'enoughness' 109–10
equality 32, 63; *see also* inequality
escapism 56
examinations 2–3

example sessions 114
exclusion 3
executives *see* CEOs
exhaustion 63, 83, 106, 109–10
eye contact 52

feedback 100–1
final reflections 119
Finnis, M. 85
friendship in Arabic culture 6

gift giving 31
Gill, Narinder 46–7
Gilligan, C. 13
goodwill 30
Greenleaf, R. K. 13
guilt 107–9

happiness 18
Harter, J. K. 13
Harvard Business Review 25, 88, 99
Harvard Business Series on Emotional Intelligence 20
headteachers 42–3, 103–16
hobbies and interests 56
honest feedback 39
honesty *ix*, 63, 86, 99, 104, 110, 114, 116
human dignity 13, 62

Ibadah (wisdom) 117–18
identity 18, 20
imposter syndrome 7
inclusion *x*, *xii*, 4, 32, 49, 90; inclusive culture 13, 29
individuality 21, 23, 32, 43
inequality 62; *see also* equality
INSET (In-service Education and Training days) 19–20, 115
integrity 104
intention 86, 110
interruption 52, 91, 92
intrinsic motivation 68–9
introspection 53–4, 71
Islam 117–18

joy 38, 55–6

key performance indicators (KPIs) 33
kindness *ix*, 24, 30, 59

Index

Kline, Nancy 4, 52, 91
Kohut, M. 25
Kuvaas, B. 67, 68

Lakhiani, V. 73–4
leadership models 104–5
limiting beliefs 93–4
loneliness 19, 22, 49–50, 103

Malcolm X 62–4
Māori culture 18–19
meetings: transforming 33–4; *see also* staff meetings
mental health *x*, 16; training 19
metaphor 12–14
micro-aggressions 4
MIQs (Most Important Questions) *xii*, 41, 44, 72, 74–9, 81, 87, 94
moral responsibility 14
morale *see* staff morale
Morris, Fiona 100
motivation 38, 50, 83–4; performance management and 67–72, 80; *see also* intrinsic motivation
multi-academy trusts (MATs) 24, 78, 87, 118
Murphy, K. R. 67, 68
Myatt, Mary 28–30
Myers, Rhys 5, 7

Nasir, Bushra 117–18
Neffinger, J. 25
negative emotion 18
Nichols, Lisa *xiii*, 85–6, 96
NPQs (National Professional Qualifications) 25

Ofsted (Office for Standards in Education, Children's Services and Skill) 5, 6, 7, 17
openness 58–61
oppression 4
organisational culture *xii*
organisational tension 87
Owen, Michael 24
oxytocin 33, 43

Palmer, Ann 12–14
people management 32

perfectionism 109
performance management *ix, xii, xii*, 6, 40–1, 65–81; accountability and 65–7, 71–2, 77, 79, 81; autonomy and 71–2; CEOs and executive team reflection 78–9; compliance-focused *xi*; definition of 65; friction 87; important questions 73–5; metrics 65–6; MIQs, power of 73–9; motivation and 67–72; personal objectives 67; purpose of 80; reinvention of *xiii*; saying 'no' 96; status quo, questioning the 66–8; theory of 65–6; *Whitechapel* case study 75–6
Perry, Ruth 6
personal growth/development *ix*, 74, 80
personal offer 115–16
perspective blindness 5
philosophical traditions 14
philosophy of education 71
physical touch 31
Plashet School (UK) 118
Porath, C. 20
positive culture 38
positive states of being 4, 16–20, 24, 34–6, 38, 53; scientific basis 33
positive to negative ratio 17
positivity *x*, 18; *see also* toxic positivity
pride 54–5
professional courtesy 39, 43
professional development 20, 70–1; policy 66; *see also* CPD (continuing professional development)
professional standards 9
professionalism 11
psychological safety *ix, xi*, 3, 6, 13, 20, 32, 54, 58, 60–1; carefrontations 88, 99; connection and 21–2, 50–1

quality: of being 53; of performance 52–3; of thinking 34, 52–3; time 31

reading 56–7
recognition 37
recruitment crisis *x*, 5, 6
reflection 113
relational systems 88–9
religion 14; *see also* Buddhism; Islam
resilience 4, 16–17, 27, 88; emotional 99; organisational *x*

125

Index

respect *x*, *xi*, 59; mutual *xiii*; respectful communication ix
results-driven approach 82–3
retention crisis *x*, 5
rounds, strategy of 52–3

Sadiz, Sufian 62–4
safeguarding 7
safety 32–3; *see also* psychological safety
satisfaction 38
saying 'no' 96–9
scheduling 110
Schein, E. H. 12
school attendance 3
school evaluation form (SEF) 16
school exclusions 3–4
Scott, Kim *xiii*, 86
Scott, S. 88
scrutiny 66
self-care: importance of *xiii*; practical guide 110–11; promotion of *xiv*; strategies ix
self-efficacy 32, 54, 111–12
self-esteem *x*
self-growth *ix*
Shetty, J. 17, 33
silence 64, 89–92, 108, 119
SLTs (Senior Leadership Teams) 40–1, 43, 76, 89, 91, 93, 97–8, 106, 110
social class 118
Special Educational Needs and Disabilities (SEND) 5
sporting organisations 19
Spreitzer, G. 20
staff meetings *xi-xii*
staff morale 23, 27, 67, 83
staff surveys 23–4, 32, 37–40
story of origin 1–11
storytelling narratives 87
stress *x*, 57
subjectivity 68
support networks 39
support structures 105–6
sustainability 96–7; sustainable performance *x*
Swart, T. 33
Syed, Matthew 5

'tangible and tactical' 17
'Teach me how to treat you': application in education 35–6; concept of *ix*, *xi*, 26, 31–45
Teacher Wellbeing Index 17
team cohesion 91–3
teamwork 38
tension: organisational 87; unspoken 89–91
testimonials 115
thinking *xii*; quality of 34, 52–3
time, forgetting about 49, 56–7
titles 104
togetherness 19
toxic positivity 17
transformational leadership 13
trauma 46, 93
trust *xiii*, 58–9, 61; mutual 107
truth 111

UK Government Keeping Children Safe in Education initiative 9
unconditional positive regard 5–6
United Nations (UN) 4

validation 16, 33, 111
value-added models 68–9
value lists 31–2
values in action 106–7
vulnerability *ix*, *x*, 1–2, 8, 11, 21, 25, 63, 87, 103, 107; connecting questions 54, 58, 61

WAGOLL (what a good one looks like) 33, 40
warmth 25, 29
wellbeing *xi*, 15–16, 19, 59; coaching 112–14; concept of 13; culture of 53, 101; 'doing' wellbeing *vs* 'being' well 16–18, 26; everyday practice 46; foundational nature of 63; scores 23–4; strategies and support *x*, *xiii*, 9, 106; supervision 6–8; systems 115; teachers 69
wellness tips 110–11
Whitechapel Church of England primary school xi, 40–4, 74–6, 78, 81
work/life balance 57–8

Yousafzai, Malala 4

For Product Safety Concerns and Information please contact our EU representative GPSR@taylorandfrancis.com
Taylor & Francis Verlag GmbH, Kaufingerstraße 24, 80331 München, Germany

www.ingramcontent.com/pod-product-compliance
Lightning Source LLC
Chambersburg PA
CBHW050911160426
43194CB00011B/2359